Heaven

Heaven

George F. Walker

Talonbooks
2000

Talonbooks
P.O. Box 2076, Vancouver, British Columbia, Canada V6B 3S3
www.talonbooks.com

Typeset in New Baskerville and printed and bound in Canada by
Hignell Printing Ltd.

Second Printing: May 2002

The publisher gratefully acknowledges the financial support of the
Canada Council for the Arts; the Government of Canada through the
Book Publishing Industry Development Program; and the Province
of British Columbia through the British Columbia Arts Council for
our publishing activities.

 Canadä

Canadian Cataloguing in Publication Data
Walker, George F., 1947-
  Heaven

  A play.
  ISBN 0-88922-429-3

  I. Title.
PS8595.A557H42 2000   C812'.54   C00-910204-3
PR9199.3.W342H42 2000

Heaven was first produced on January 15, 2000 at the Canadian Stage Theatre in Toronto, Ontario with the following cast:

JIMMY	Ron White
JUDY / KARLETTE	Nola Augustson
KARL	Wayne Best
DAVID	Michael Spencer-Davis
DEREK	Joel Gordon
SISSY / KARLETTE	Samantha Reynolds

Directed by George F. Walker
Associate Director: Dani Romain
Set and Costume Design: Shawn Kerwin
Lighting Design: Kevin Fraser
Sound Design: Henry Monteforte
Fight Director: John Stead
Choreographer: Sara Brenner
Circus Coach: Greg Tarlin
Stage Manager: Naomi Campbell
Apprentice Stage Manager: Helen Himsl

Persons

JAMES JOYCE MILLIKEN (JIMMY)

JUDY GARSON

KARL SMITH

DAVID OLSHEN

DEREK

SISSY

Place

A city park. Several benches. Lots of trees. A gravel pathway. Part of a church wall. Against another wall, some scaffolding, a dumpster.

And in the background, a city street.

And beyond that, a cityscape.

Prologue

Edge of a city park.
KARL waiting. Smoking. Sports jacket. Open collar.
Unshaven.
JIMMY comes on. Hands in pockets.

KARL

Thanks for coming.

JIMMY

Yeah well we gotta make it fast. I've got a family
dinner.

KARL

No it's okay. I don't need long. Thanks for coming.
Did I say that.

JIMMY

Yeah.

KARL

I'm kinda messed up.

JIMMY

Yeah.

KARL

Is that all you can say, Jimmy. I say I'm kinda
messed up. And you say "yeah."

JIMMY

You got something in mind for me to say.

KARL

I'm just telling you I'm not in great shape and I
want you to say more than yeah and nod like a
fucking dog.

7

JIMMY
    Get to it.

KARL
    Get to what.

JIMMY
    Why I'm here. What you want.

KARL
    You need to know something. You need to know
    something about Tommy.

JIMMY
    Yeah? What?

KARL
    He's dead.

JIMMY
    Whatya mean he's dead.

KARL
    He's dead. You killed him. Well he pulled the
    trigger. He put the gun to his head and pulled the
    fucking trigger. But really you killed him. I'm
    blaming you.

JIMMY
    When did this happen.

KARL
    Last night I guess. They found him this morning.

JIMMY
    His family?

KARL
    Yeah. His family. His kids. His kids found him. You
    prick. (*grabs JIMMY*) You rotten prick.

JIMMY
    Let me go … Get your fucking hands off me.

KARL steps back

JIMMY

   Look ... I'm sorry about Tommy.

KARL

   I'm blaming you.

JIMMY

   I was doing my job.

KARL

   You ruined his life.

JIMMY

   He killed that kid. He was a fuckup. He shouldn't
   have been a cop anyway. Taking his badge away was
   a thing that should have happened years ago.

KARL

   Says who.

JIMMY

   Me.

KARL

   You're an asshole, Jimmy. A heartless murdering
   asshole. He was your friend! You'd known him
   since you were five fucking years old. You know his
   mother and his father. You've eaten food off their
   table. Maybe some part of your cold heartless brain
   could have remembered that while you were doing
   your fucking "job."

JIMMY

   He killed that kid because he was black.

KARL

   Bullshit. Tommy had nothing against blacks.

JIMMY

   Nothing except he thought they were all criminals.
   He saw that kid in that stairwell and there was no

9

benefit of the doubt, Karl. He just pulled the trigger.

KARL

Bullshit. The kid looked like he was gonna—

JIMMY

Look. Shut the fuck up.

KARL

(*pulls a gun from his shoulder holster*) No you shut the fuck up. Mr. Bigshot lawyer. Mr. Protect every asshole in the whole fucking world. Protect everyone except his friends. Mr. Human Rights. What a bunch of crap. Human rights. Two things. One, what are rights. The right to fuck up and rape and mug and kill. And two, who says they're human. Really. I mean really.

(KARL has the gun at JIMMY's head)

JIMMY

Put that away.

KARL

Yeah. But first I think I'll use it.

JIMMY

Use it? On me?

KARL

On you. On me. What's it matter. I'm messed up. But I think really so are you. I mean you gotta be. You've forgotten where you're from, man. You're wandering around in a strange world without loyalty. You're disconnected. You're pathetic.

JIMMY

No. You're pathetic.

JIMMY pushes KARL away.

KARL

I'll kill you you son of a bitch.

JIMMY

I'm going home.

KARL

He was our friend! He was my partner!! And he was a good cop! And you never blinked when it came time to take him down. You just compiled a shitload of "factual" evidence and fucked him over royally ... He was ... my friend! (*sinks to the ground*) He was my friend you son of a bitch!!

KARL is weeping.
JIMMY is gone.
Blackout.

11

Scene One

Dusk.
City park.
Skyscrapers loom in the background.
*JAMES JOYCE MILLIKEN—they call him JIMMY—is
sitting on a bench taking swigs from a magnum of
champagne. He's wearing a nice suit but he is kind
of messed up. His tie is undone. One of his sleeves is
a bit ripped and he has a cut over an eye.*
*On the other side of the park, under a park lamp
which acts as a kind of overhead spot light, SISSY is
practising juggling three hackysacks. She is not very
good. But she is trying hard. She is about sixteen.
Pierced. Ragged. Wiry.*
*JIMMY watches her intently. Occasionally he checks to
see if his cut is still bleeding, licking the blood off his
fingers each time.*

SISSY
    Fuck.

    SISSY has dropped a hackysack.

SISSY
    Fuck.

    She picks it up. Juggles. Drops one.

SISSY
    Fuck. You little fuckers.

    She picks it up. Juggles. Drops one.

SISSY
    Fuck.

    She picks it up. Juggles. Drops one.

SISSY

Fuck.

She picks it up. Juggles. Drops all three.

SISSY

Fuck. Fuck it. I fucking give up.

JUDY GARSON passes SISSY as she is bending down for her hackysack. JUDY is dressed in overcoat and high heels. And in a hurry.

SISSY

Got any change?

JUDY

(*without stopping*) No.

SISSY

Are you sure ... Hey!

JUDY

(*stops, turns*) What.

SISSY

Are you sure. I mean you didn't even look.

JUDY

Don't say "hey" when a person walks by. If a person says no and keeps walking that's okay. There's nothing wrong with that. Just let the person go. Don't say "hey." It sounds threatening. A person doesn't need to feel threatened in a situation like this. Okay?

SISSY

Sure.

JUDY

Good.

JUDY starts off.

SISSY
    Hey!

> JUDY stops. Turns.

SISSY
    Sorry.

> SISSY leaves.
> JUDY continues over to JIMMY.

JIMMY
    Why didn't you give her some money.

JUDY
    I don't have any on me.

JIMMY
    (mumbles) Bullshit.

JUDY
    What did you say. Did you just say bullshit.

JIMMY
    You've got your shoe money. Twenty dollars in each
    shoe.

JUDY
    I don't do that anymore.

JIMMY
    (mumbles) Bullshit.

JUDY
    Did you just say bullshit again.

JIMMY
    You don't do that anymore. Gimme a break. Take
    your shoes off.

JUDY
    I'm not taking my shoes off.

JIMMY
    Why not.

JUDY

> Because I don't want to. Because I don't take my shoes off just because someone tells me to. Who the hell are you to tell me to take my shoes off.

JIMMY

> Take off your shoes.

JUDY

> Fuck off!

JIMMY

> Take off your shoes and show me those two sad little twenty dollar bills you always put in when you're going out just in case the Gestapo grabs you and you'll have something to bribe a camp guard with.

JUDY

> You lowlife working class anti-Semitic prick. The next time you make one of those fucking stupid Gestapo cracks to me I'm gonna deck you. I mean it Jimmy. I'll smash you right in your stupid drunken face.

JIMMY

> Why didn't you give her any money.

JUDY

> Why'd you leave the party.

JIMMY

> All you had to do was take off a shoe. She needs that twenty a hell of a lot more than you do. If the Gestapo is coming for anyone these days, honey, it's her. Not you. I'm sorry I said Gestapo. It just slipped out.

JUDY

> Why'd you leave the party.

JIMMY

Aren't you gonna ask me why I'm bleeding.

JUDY

Why are you bleeding.

JIMMY

I left the party because I overheard you talking to your mother in the kitchen.

JUDY

Why are you bleeding. What did you hear.

JIMMY

I fell down the stairs. I heard you talking about getting an abortion.

JUDY

What? What were you doing. Were you listening at the door.

JIMMY

I just fucking said I was listening at the door.

JUDY

You said you overheard. That's a little different than admitting you were spying on us.

JIMMY

Well you know, when I see you and your mother head off for one of those little conferences I've found over the years it's best to have an idea of what's going on before the nuclear device lands on my fucking head. I thought Jews were against abortion.

JUDY

What do you know what Jews are for or against.

JIMMY

Hey I read the pamphlets. They're all over the
goddamn house, Judy. Support Israel. Propagate
the chosen ones.

JUDY

Right. So. What. You hear us talking about a
hypothetical thing. I'm talking to my mother about
some concerns I have. I'm explaining some
possible options and you just get in some ugly little
Jew-hating temper and storm out of the apartment.

JIMMY

Actually I accidentally bumped into Sid on my way
out and he called me a few names which were
intended to defame my Irish heritage and my
Roman faith. Then he threw me down the stairs.

JUDY

Sid? Who the hell is Sid?

JIMMY

Sid. Your rabbi.

JUDY

His name is David, asshole. What the hell is wrong
with you, calling him Sid.

JIMMY

Sid. David. What the fuck's it matter. How does he
feel about abortion is all I want to know. Have you
talked it over with him. I mean he didn't say
something like it's too bad we can't just abort the
heathen Irish part and keep the Jewish part. Just in
case.

JUDY

Just in case what.

17

JIMMY

Just in case the little half breed's the fucking
messiah. Don't tell me that's not a concern, Judy.

JUDY

You are like the world's biggest asshole.

JIMMY

That's my child inside you Judy. You shouldn't be
talking to *anybody* about killing it except me.

JUDY

I tried to talk to you about it. You got stupid. You
said stupid things, remember.

JIMMY

I think all I said was that in my family it—

JUDY

Fuck your family. Fuck your family's religious
beliefs.

JIMMY

I wasn't talking about my family's religious beliefs. I
was just saying that they've got some pretty strong
feelings about—

JUDY

Yeah, right. It's not religious. It's about "strong
feelings." Their long tradition of yacking about
the sanctity of life. And all this crap about my
religion—it's not related in any way to your family's
ugly little history of Jew hating through the ages.
Oh no.

JIMMY

Listen. I'm just talking about—

JUDY

And speaking of your family. I really don't want to
hear what they think about anything. Those

ignorant bigoted creeps. All they've ever done is exclude me and suggest in every sneaky little way they could find that I just married you because you were a lawyer.

JIMMY

Gee, Judy. Whose mother was almost orgasmic because her daughter was marrying a lawyer. I mean a lawyer to your mother, what's that. The next best thing to a doctor.

JUDY

She liked you, you jerk. Because you left that assembly line, went back to school and made something of yourself. She liked you for all the reasons I liked you. When I liked you.

JIMMY

Ah fuck this garbage. All I wanna know is, what's gonna happen to my child.

JUDY

Well fuck whatever you want to know. It's my body. My life. I'll do whatever I want with both of them.

JIMMY

I'm your husband.

JUDY

You're a drunken idiot. And I don't want to talk to you anymore

She starts off.

JIMMY

Where you going.

JUDY

Home.

JIMMY

I'm not coming.

JUDY

Like I give a shit.

She leaves.
He sits.
He drinks.
He stands. Starts after her. Stops.

JIMMY

(*yelling*) Okay. That's it. Everything has to be
rethought. I thought we had an agreement. I
thought we had a life based on an agreement. I
guess not.

JUDY comes back on.

JUDY

Are you coming home.

JIMMY

Do I look like I'm coming home, Judy.

JUDY

I think you should.

JIMMY

You're a liar. When people ask me about you from
now on I'm going to tell them that. "What's Judy
like." "She's a liar."

JUDY

I'm forty-two years old, Jimmy. I can't have another
child.

JIMMY

Let me remind you of the agreement. The
agreement went something like this. Neither of
us would let our stupid careers or our mutual
tendency toward self-absorption deter us from a
commitment to our family.

JUDY

This has nothing to do with my stupid career.

JIMMY

It has everything to do with your stupid career.
How can a pregnant woman spend five months in a
rain forest watching larvae produce antioxidants.

JUDY

Oh you asshole. That was just me speculating. No
one's ever done a real time documentary in a rain
forest. It's just a thought that came to me. Like I'm
really going to do it or something.

JIMMY

Do it. Don't do it. Go make a documentary about
sexual abuse in a Ukrainian hockey league. Go film
the senseless slaughter of the wild ostrich. I don't
care. You're a liar. You broke the agreement. Fuck
off ...

JUDY

Okay. See you.

She starts off.

JIMMY

Maybe.

JUDY

Asshole.

DEREK and JUDY pass each other. DEREK is
twenty-five. He is SISSY's mentor.

DEREK

Hi. Sorry to bother you. Could you spare a little
something.

JUDY

No!

JIMMY
    Liar!

    JUDY leaves. DEREK goes over to JIMMY.

DEREK
    Hi.

JIMMY
    Hi.

DEREK
    Nice night.

JIMMY
    Yeah. Great.

DEREK
    Got any change?

JIMMY
    So much for small talk, eh ... Yeah. Here.

    He gives DEREK a twenty dollar bill.

JIMMY
    That's a twenty dollar bill.

DEREK
    Yeah. I can see that.

JIMMY
    Do you know why I'm giving you twenty dollars.

DEREK
    Not really.

JIMMY
    Because it's important to me that I feel I'm a more
    superior human being than that woman who just
    left.

DEREK
    Why stop at twenty, man. If you give me fifty you
    could feel like her fucking God.

JIMMY

(*laughs*) Her fucking God. That's good. But her fucking God is awesome. He is one awesome unforgiving wrathful guy. I can't get near that kind of emotional power. I've got a God thing that's more lightweight. A few candles drink his son's blood kind of thing.

DEREK

That's a large bottle you're drinking from. I mean the way you're talking now I gotta think if you finish that bottle you're gonna be unconscious.

JIMMY

Then what happens? You steal my clothes and slit my throat?

DEREK throws his hands up. Backs off.

DEREK

Hey man. That was not a necessary thing to say.

JIMMY

Oh. Did I offend you.

DEREK

Yeah you fucking offended me.

JIMMY

Oh. Well. I'm sorry. Don't know where that came from. I mean white guys who dress like me hardly ever get murdered in parks by black kids anymore.

DEREK

Thanks for the money.

JIMMY

You still look offended.

DEREK

Look you're drunk, okay. And I gotta go ... 'cause
I'm looking for someone and I don't want to get
into anything with you. I really don't.

JIMMY

Who you looking for.

DEREK

A girl. I think she was coming here.

JIMMY

Tiny girl. Plaid vest. Lots of ... pierced ... things.

DEREK

Yeah ... And she might have been doing something
weird.

JIMMY

She was juggling ... sort of.

DEREK

Juggling. Yeah, fuck. Man when is she gonna get it.
She never gets it. Thinks she can teach herself so
she can ... I don't know ... She's such a—

JIMMY

You're not going to call her a bitch are you.

DEREK

What.

JIMMY

I don't like that. That bitch ho stuff. It sickens me.

DEREK

I was just gonna say—

JIMMY

Because it's like you're saying she's just some
pathetic piece of trash and you're a Nubian prince
or something.

DEREK
Nubian? That's a black comment isn't it. You're
fucking with me right. Nubian is some kind of
replacement word for nigger, right.

JIMMY
Hey if I was the kind of guy who used the word
nigger why would I need a replacement word.

DEREK
I don't know. Maybe so I wouldn't kick your head
in or something.

JIMMY
I was just saying it's not nice for you to be calling
young girls bitches.

DEREK gets close to JIMMY.

DEREK
You hear me call her a bitch? Did the word bitch
come outta my mouth. I was just gonna say how
she's not being real that's all. She gets these ideas
that aren't real, so if you're a friend of hers, a
person who cares about her, you can get kinda
frustrated and, you know, worried.

JIMMY
What's your name.

DEREK
Why do you need to know my name.

JIMMY
What's your name.

DEREK
I'm not telling you my fucking name.

JIMMY
My name is Jimmy.

DEREK

I don't give a shit what your name is.

JIMMY

What's your name.

DEREK

Look shut the fuck up. You're starting to really
irritate me. You irritate me anymore and I'm gonna
get rambunctious.

JIMMY

Rambunctious. That's good. But what's it mean.
Does it mean you're gonna hit me. I can't see
anything good coming to either of us if you do
that. I mean here we are just talking. Okay there
are things we disagree about. But does that mean
we have to start hitting each other. Are we fucking
animals!! Are we!! (*advancing*) Are we!!

DEREK

Hey. Back off!

JIMMY

What's your fucking name!

DEREK

Derek!

JIMMY

What?

DEREK

Derek.

JIMMY

Spell it!

DEREK

Fuck off!

JIMMY
> What's wrong. Can't you spell your own name, you
> stupid fucking Nubian.
>
> *DEREK punches him in the stomach. JIMMY drops.*

JIMMY
> Ah fuck that hurt. Hey why aren't you running.
> You're ... supposed to run. That's why they call it
> hit and run Derek.

DEREK
> I ... wanna make sure you're okay.

JIMMY
> Really.

DEREK
> I mean I'm sorry. But man you—

JIMMY
> What's wrong. How come you can't take a little
> aggressive provocation. Didn't they teach you how
> to deal with that in your "How to Survive as a
> Visible Minority in a Hostile White Culture" class
> you took. Well did you take the fucking course or
> not.

DEREK
> Yeah I guess I fucking took it.

JIMMY
> He guesses he took it. Hey. I know you took the
> course. You know how. I designed it asshole. That's
> right. I designed it. You took it second year of high
> school.

DEREK
> They called it something else.

JIMMY
> I let them call it what they needed to call it, Derek.

DEREK

> Something like "Integration with Power and Integrity" or some stupid shit.

JIMMY

> Integration with power? No fucking way. Who called it that.

DEREK

> My teacher.

JIMMY

> Fucking teachers. Idiots.

DEREK

> You're not a teacher?

JIMMY

> Lawyer.

DEREK

> Lawyer? So how come you made up a course they had in high school.

JIMMY

> I'm a lawyer ... with ... I think you broke a rib ... I'm a lawyer with the government. Human rights commission. I'm in charge of minority rights. (*laughs*) I'm very big in minority rights.

DEREK

> No way. And you're calling me that Nubian shit. That's a replacement word. I'm sure of it.

JIMMY

> Hey we're making progress, baby. My father never used replacement words. He used nigger, baby. He used nigger, wop, polack, kike. He used them all ... Ah fuck I can barely breathe. Look I gotta ask you something ... If I pass out and you're inspired to kill me, could you place an anonymous phone call

to the police. I don't want my kids wondering what happened to me okay? Look I'm sorry I keep saying things like that to you. You know things that suggest you're a piece of criminal garbage. I don't know what's wrong with me. I mean look at me. I've had a rough night. I'm really fucking drunk now. And well I had a serious personal altercation earlier that I think has left some deep emotional scars.

DEREK

I gotta go. I … I gotta find Sissy.

JIMMY

Sissy? Oh yeah. The juggler. She yo bitch? (*laughs*) Sorry. Really. You know Derek I gotta wonder about how sensitive a guy you are though. I mean we've been talking all this time. I give you twenty bucks, and you ever once enquired how come I look all fucked up like this.

DEREK

I was going to. It was almost the first thing that occurred to me. But then you started irritating me and I forgot.

JIMMY

My wife's rabbi beat me up. Cocksucker hates Catholics. The only thing he hates more than Catholics is Palestinians. When he found out I was a Catholic Palestinian sympathizer there was no restraining him. He threw me down a flight of stairs. Calmly walked down. Stood over me awhile grinning like the lunatic Zionist he is. Then stomped on my face till it bled.

DEREK

A rabbi? Shit. Man, is that the truth.

JIMMY

It's the story I'm telling.

DEREK

Yeah. Well ...

JIMMY

You gotta go.

DEREK

Yeah ... See you.

DEREK is backing off.

JIMMY

My wife's getting an abortion.

DEREK

Really.

JIMMY

Yeah ... She says it's because she's old. She thinks I think it's because she loves her career. It's not though. She just doesn't want another baby with me. She hates my guts.

DEREK

(*leaving*) That's too bad.

JIMMY

My marriage is pretty well over.

DEREK

Later, okay?

DEREK is gone.

JIMMY

Yeah. My marriage is in the crapper. And also. I think a piece of that rib has pierced my heart. And I'm going into ... (*falls to his knees*) cardiac arrest.

He groans.

JIMMY

Oh shit ... I'm in trouble here.

Groans.

Collapses on his face.

Blackout.

Siren.

Scene Two

KARL is chasing DEREK. DEREK is yelling stuff like "fuck off," "leave me alone," and swerving behind trees and benches. KARL is looking pretty rough, in an old coat, dirty, unshaven. He is laughing and breathing really hard.

KARL

You fucking stay put you little prick. You make me do this much longer and I'm gonna have to kill you or something. (*laughs*)

DEREK

Just go away, man. Just leave me alone, okay.

KARL

Come here.

DEREK

No.

KARL

Come here right fucking now.

DEREK

No way.

KARL

You stupid little piece of shit. I'm gonna rip open your throat.

DEREK

Leave me alone. You're crazy, man. Just leave me alone!!

DEREK takes off. But KARL, by leaping over a bench, intercepts and tackles him.

DEREK

Ah fuck.

They are rolling around.

KARL

Hey I got you now. I got you, sweetheart. You just stay put. Stop squirming. I said stay put. (*hits him*) I told you not to squirm, asshole.

DEREK

Ah man. You ... Fuck that hurt.

KARL is dragging DEREK to a bench.

DEREK

You gotta be the biggest ... Man ... man you're hurting me.

KARL

Shut up.

DEREK

What are you doing. Where you taking me.

KARL

Shut up.

KARL takes out some handcuffs.

DEREK

No way. Whatya doin'.

KARL

Shut up.

KARL is handcuffing DEREK to a bench.

DEREK

Don't do this. I hate this. This isn't happenin'. No way.

DEREK tries to escape.

KARL

Shut up. You had your chance to do this in a much
more civilized manner. You decided to run. Now
what's this.

He takes out a police detective's badge.

KARL

I said what is this. Is this a policeman's badge.

DEREK

Yeah, but—

KARL kicks him.

KARL

Is it or is it not a badge.

DEREK

Yeah. Yeah it is but—

KARL

But what, you piece of shit. Did you run or not?
Did I have to chase you or not. Are you a stupid
little prick or aren't you. So just be quiet. Tell
yourself to get docile and let it happen. Or I'm
really gonna hurt you. Get it? Here hold this for a
while.

He stuffs the badge into DEREK's mouth.
KARL gets DEREK handcuffed to the bench.

KARL

Good boy. Wow. That was ugly. (*he sits*) Wasn't it.
Plain ugly ... I'm surprised at how mean and low
my behaviour can sink ... Almost inexcusable.
Barbaric ... Barbaric and sad ... I mean something
happens. It just happens in a certain way that pisses
me off and I just go to this ugly place ... This fuck
you and die in your pain place ... I blame you,
Derek. You and others like you. You've turned me

34

into a fucking monster. I'm just almost pure anger.
I'm not fit to be with civilized people. I can't go
home anymore. I can't be with my family ... I'm not
fit ... Yeah I'm not fit and I blame you, you little
piece of shit ... Some day I'm gonna have to kill
you for what you've done to me. Really. Some day
... I'll take that now.

He takes the badge from DEREK's mouth.

KARL

Thanks ... Now where were we. You know before
things got ugly and you ran ... Oh yeah. I said "Hi
Derek, got that thing I wanted?" ... So ... (*cuffs him
on the head*) Hi Derek. Got that thing I wanted?

DEREK

Look you gotta loosen these cuffs. They hurt.

KARL

Got that thing I wanted? I sure do want that thing.
You got it? (*close to his face*) You got it, Derek?

DEREK

I got it! Yeah!

KARL

You got it?

DEREK

I got it ... It's ... ah ... I got it though.

KARL

Though. What's that mean! I got it though.

DEREK

It's not with me. I've got it somewhere else.

KARL

Somewhere else? There is no somewhere else
Derek. There's only here. You telling me you living
somewhere now?

35

DEREK

No I'm not living somewhere. *It's* somewhere
though. It's *with* someone who's living somewhere.

KARL

So you don't "got it"? Someone else has got it.

DEREK

Someone else I can get it from. So I got it when I
get it from this someone.

KARL

You've seen it.

DEREK

I've seen it. I've touched it. It's a Glock right. Got a
little nick in the handle. What? You hit someone in
the head who had a steel plate or something?

KARL

Was that a joke, Derek. You making a joke at my
expense?

DEREK

It wasn't a joke, man. I'm just wondering how you
got a little piece missing from your gun.

KARL

Did I say it was *my* gun.

DEREK

I thought it was.

KARL

Fuck what you think. I never ever fucking want to
hear what you think. Now did I ever say it was mine.
Did you ever hear me refer to that gun as
something that belonged to me.

DEREK

Yes.

KARL

Yes?

DEREK
    No?
KARL
    No. Good. So where is it. So where's this person
    live who's got it.
DEREK
    He wants money.
KARL
    I gave you money.
DEREK
    He wants more.
KARL
    How much more.
DEREK
    He wants another five hundred dollars.
KARL
    So all together he wants a thousand.
DEREK
    Yeah.
KARL
    Because you've already given him five hundred, right.
DEREK
    Yeah.
KARL
    Except you didn't. You put that five hundred
    dollars in your bloodstream didn't you.
DEREK
    No.
KARL
    Didn't you!?

DEREK
No!

> KARL *pulls his gun. Puts it under* DEREK's *chin.*

KARL
Didn't you!?

DEREK
Yes! Yes!!

KARL
Yes ... I don't think you have the proper respect for me, son. I've failed you in that regard. It appears you think I can be trifled with. Why is that. Is it my engaging smile. My low-key sense of humour? What? What would make you spend that money on drugs and think there wouldn't be consequences, you fucking idiot.

DEREK
I didn't care about the consequences man! I'm a drug addict. Jesus. Who's the fucking idiot.

KARL
What.

DEREK
Nothing ... Nothing!

KARL
Fuck it. I need that gun. I need you to get that gun.

> KARL *unlocks the cuffs.*

DEREK
Yeah so give me another five hundred and it's yours.

KARL
Yeah sure we'll really be going down that road again. No. I think we'll do it this way. You just go get it from the guy.

DEREK

Without money?

KARL

That's right.

DEREK

How am I gonna do that. I'd have to kill him to get that gun off him, man.

KARL

Oh. Okay.

DEREK

Okay what.

KARL

Kill him.

DEREK

You want me to kill him.

KARL

Yeah.

DEREK

Jesus … I mean … Jesus.

KARL

Hey come on. It was your idea.

DEREK

I can't.

KARL

Sure you can.

DEREK

No. No way. I'm not like that.

KARL

Like what.

DEREK

I'm not a killer.

KARL

Fuck off. "I'm not a killer." So what are you. You're
a pimping piece of drug taking lying stealing shit.
But you're not a killer. Because why, you got
principles? Fuck off. I mean it. Get going. You've
got till sunup. Get going. I mean it. (*advancing*) I
want that gun. And I want that guy who's got that
gun dead!! Come on. Get going. Fuck off, asshole!!
I mean it!!

DEREK turns. Runs.
KARL sits. Lights a smoke.
Blackout.

Scene Three

SISSY on a unicycle. Holding on to various things,
she crosses the park and then back again.
DAVID is watching her from a bench.
JUDY pushes JIMMY on in a wheelchair. JIMMY waves
at SISSY as she passes by again. SISSY waves back.
JUDY pushes JIMMY over to DAVID.

JUDY
  Sorry we're late.

DAVID
  It's okay.

JUDY
  We had to talk about something.

DAVID
  I understand.

  SISSY passes by on her unicycle.

JIMMY
  You understand what.

JUDY
  He understands why we were late.

JIMMY
  No he understands that we had had to talk about
  something. (*to DAVID*) What was it.

DAVID
  What was what. I'm sorry. I don't understand what
  you're—

JIMMY
  What do you think we were talking about.

DAVID
    I don't know.

    JIMMY gestures helplessness.

JIMMY
    Liars. I'm surrounded by liars.

JUDY
    Listen, David. Maybe today's not good for this.

JIMMY
    Today's fine.

DAVID
    (*to JIMMY*) I just thought we could talk. But if you're
    not feeling—

JIMMY
    We can talk.

JUDY
    But maybe not today. Maybe it's too soon.

JIMMY
    Too soon. Too late. What's it matter. Sid wants to
    talk. I'll talk. I don't know why you've even got an
    opinion about it, Jude. You can just leave.

JUDY
    I don't mind staying.

JIMMY
    But it's me Sid wants to talk to.

JUDY
    Stop calling him Sid, Jimmy.

JIMMY
    If he wanted me to stop calling him Sid don't you
    think he'd say something.

DAVID
    My name's not Sid, Jimmy. My name is David.

JIMMY
Sure it is.

JUDY
Ah shit. You said you'd be nice.

JIMMY
Did I actually use the word "nice." Doesn't sound like me.

DAVID
Judy. Why don't you just leave us alone for awhile. Jimmy and I will have our little chat. Then you can come back and take him home.

JUDY
Are you sure.

DAVID
We'll be fine.

JUDY
Okay ... I'll go ...

JIMMY
Go shopping. Buy something nice.

JUDY
I don't need anything.

JIMMY
I meant for me ... Jesus. Come on, Jude. A little thoughtfulness. I mean who almost died. Who could use a little ... you know ... gesture of kindness or something.

JUDY
I'll get something for supper.

She leaves.
They watch her.

JIMMY
A good looking woman, isn't she.

DAVID
Yes. She is.

JIMMY
She gives amazing head.

DAVID
Really. And why would you think I'd need to have that information.

JIMMY
Well there's a lot of anti-Semitic propaganda out there about how Jewish women don't like to perform oral sex. And I thought you might like to hear first-hand how that's not really true. I mean since you probably don't have any personal experience I was just—

DAVID
Okay let's get a few things clear first. Then maybe we can talk about what's going on in your marriage.

JIMMY
How about we get a few things clear then maybe we *don't* talk about what's going on in my marriage

SISSY cycles on. Gets off. Starts juggling her hackysacks.

JIMMY
Six weeks ago she couldn't do that. I mean none of it. Not the unicycle. Not the juggling.

DAVID
Really.

SISSY
Shit.

She has forgotten something. She drops the hackysacks
and runs off.

JIMMY

Yeah, Sid. But she ... persevered, I guess is the
word.

DAVID

First of all, Jimmy. Stop calling me Sid. It's stupid.
And it's a bit ugly ... Second I want you to stop
telling people that I beat you up. I'm a rabbi. Most
people take the story with a grain of salt
considering its source, but still—

JIMMY

She swallows too. I left that part out. She sucks. She
swallows. I think she likes the taste too.

DAVID

What's wrong with you.

JIMMY

I almost died six weeks ago.

DAVID

What was wrong with you ten weeks ago.

JIMMY

I don't know. But it got a hell of a lot worse four
weeks later. Do you mind if I ask you a question
before you start giving me all that bullshit advice
about how to save my marriage.

DAVID

I doubt very much that your marriage can be saved.
I wanted to just ask you to stop making it so hard
for Judy to return to her people.

JIMMY

Sure. No problem. But before we get into that.
What are your thoughts on heaven. I mean this

near death experience has got me mildly
interested. I know the Christian take. And wow!
Serious bullshit. But your group seems to be all
over the place on the afterlife. Some of you treat it
like it's a big deal. Some of you have never even
thought about it. There's some stuff in the Torah
which I think is actually way fucking beyond human
comprehension and then there's—

DAVID
Well right now, the only thought I have about
heaven is I hope it's somewhere I won't have to talk
to you.

 DAVID stands.

JIMMY
What are you doing.

DAVID
I'm leaving. Is that all right with you.

JIMMY
Definitely.

DAVID
I think you need to see someone about your anger.

JIMMY
Like I haven't heard that one before. I find my
anger comforting. I won't be "seeing" anyone about
it. But here's some advice for you. Stay the fuck
away from my family.

DAVID
If Judy needs me, I'll be there.

JIMMY
I was talking about my kids.

DAVID
I've never been allowed near your children, Jimmy.

JIMMY

Is it true that you advised Judy to get an abortion.

DAVID

Are you insane.

JIMMY

Is it true that in your heart you only want to abort the Irish Catholic part of the fetus. I mean if you could determine exactly what and where that was.

DAVID

What *is* wrong with you.

JIMMY

I'm hurt. I know you've never liked me and I don't understand why.

DAVID

I never had anything against you until you started acting like a demented fool. I was against your marriage that's all.

JIMMY

Against it? Is that what you call it. You were a fucking pain in the ass. We loved each other. Get it? And all we heard was this crap coming from these two ancient tribes we were trying to escape. Your fucking synagogue was almost vibrating with collective distaste. And my old man died well, basically in a bigoted rage. The Catholic way. The Jewish way. All the ways. Fuck you. Fuck your people. Fuck your ways. My marriage isn't fucked because of her career, or my callous ways, it's from fifteen years of trying to keep all you assholes at arm's length … Gee Sid you look upset. You're not gonna hit me again are you.

DAVID

You should get counselling.

DAVID starts off.

JIMMY

You should get a fucking job. A real one. And you should get it in the real world!! (*grimaces*) Oh great ... Now I'm upset. (*reaches into his pocket, takes out a bottle of pills, takes two*)

> *SISSY runs back on with a sleeping bag and begins gathering up her other belongings which are stowed around the park ... a knapsack ... some food ...*

JIMMY

Hi.

SISSY

Hi.

JIMMY

Got any change?

SISSY

What.

JIMMY

Anything will do.

SISSY

You're kidding right.

JIMMY

How's Derek.

SISSY

You know Derek?

JIMMY

He did this to me.

SISSY

No way.

JIMMY

Well … it was my fault. I provoked him. I'd like to talk to him. Where is he.

SISSY

I don't know. Around. What's wrong with you anyway.

JIMMY

I had a heart attack.

SISSY

Really. Aren't you sort of young for that.

JIMMY

Oh aren't you kind.

SISSY

I guess you don't smoke.

JIMMY

Well you're guessin' wrong, sister.

JIMMY takes a pack of cigarettes out of his pocket. Throws them to her.

JIMMY

You're doing great on that thing. And you can juggle. That's pretty impressive.

SISSY

Yeah. Well it took time.

JIMMY

Not really. I know people who've been trying to learn to juggle for years. Of course they're all middle-aged idiots who also enjoy climbing walls in gymnasiums.

SISSY

Well at first I thought "this is never gonna fuckin' happen." Then something clicked. Maybe I've got a knack. Hope so. I need to prepare.

JIMMY
  For what.

SISSY
  Begging's a drag. You know? And squeegee is
  nothing but hassle now. But I saw these guys last
  summer. Buskers? They were doing okay.

JIMMY
  So you decided ... to ... just ...

SISSY
  Yeah I decided.

JIMMY
  That's ... great. Good for you.

SISSY
  Thanks.

JIMMY
  You make me think life is worth living.

SISSY
  Yeah, right.

JIMMY
  I mean in theory ... . So where'd you get the
  unicycle?

SISSY
  Stole it.

JIMMY
  Yeah? ... Well I still think it's great.

  DEREK rushes into the park.

DEREK
  Hey! What the fuck you doin'. Come on.

  He starts off.

SISSY

    Hey come back here. Some of this stuff is yours, asshole.

DEREK

    Ah fuck.

    He helps her finish gathering the stuff and tie the knapsacks to the unicycle.

JIMMY

    Hey, Derek. Come on over here.

DEREK

    Maybe later. (*to SISSY*) What is all this shit. Come on. We gotta go.

SISSY

    I'm tryin' to go.

JIMMY

    Go where.

    DEREK is frantically picking up the unicycle and stuff. SISSY has run off to some corner to retrieve another hidden personal object.

DEREK

    What are you doin' in that chair, man.

JIMMY

    Well my mother found out my wife was thinking of getting an abortion. She figured it was my idea, seeing how little respect I have for human life. So she wrote to His Eminence in Rome asking for advice. And he had a couple of Vatican goons come over and beat the crap outta me.

DEREK

    You're a trip, man.

JIMMY

    I want to talk to you, Derek. Really.

DEREK
> But we gotta go. We got a kinda problem. There's a guy we need to get away from.

> > *SISSY runs back on ... putting a small plastic bag of dope in her pocket.*

SISSY
> Karl, right?

JIMMY
> Who.

DEREK
> (*to SISSY*) We gotta get somewhere he can't find us.

> > *They start off.*

JIMMY
> Wait! Maybe I can help.

DEREK
> It's okay ... (*to SISSY*) Come on.

> > *They run off.*
> > *SISSY has left her hackysacks on the ground. JIMMY stands and weakly walks over. Picks them up.*
> > *JUDY comes on.*

JUDY
> What are you doing.

JIMMY
> Nothing.

JUDY
> Who said you could leave the chair.

JIMMY
> David advised me to get some exercise.

JUDY
> He did?

JIMMY

I think his exact words were "Fuck off and die." But I know he really just meant for me to get some kind of exercise.

JUDY

Where is he.

JIMMY

I think he probably took his minivan to the car wash. It's Wednesday. They do minivans half-price on Wednesday.

JUDY

Fuck off. (*gives the wheelchair a violent push*) You're never going to stop, right.

JIMMY

When I'm dead. Or when I'm happy.
Whichever comes first. Or I suppose they could come simultaneously. But it's true about the minivans. The Cambodian car wash is trying to put the Vietnamese car wash out of business. Those little peckers can make a war outta just about anything.

JUDY

Suppose I was taping you. You know just recording all these random thoughts you have on minority religions and cultures. All the things they believe in. All the things you think are crap.

JIMMY

If only they just believed, eh. If only they didn't feel this urgent need to spread the crap around.

JUDY

Anyway suppose I had these tapes and I took them
into your bosses, and said "Hey boys. Listen to this.
Here's the guy in charge of all your human rights
complaints."

JIMMY

Have you ever given a blowjob to someone in a
wheelchair.

JUDY

You don't think it'd concern them a little. They
don't know about your private battle against
everything that isn't honest and real. They don't
know about your unofficial campaign to eradicate
all the bullshit from the world. The black bullshit,
the gay bullshit, the Muslim, the Jewish bullshit.

JIMMY

The Christian bullshit too. Come on. Fair is fair.

JUDY

Oh yeah, I know. You thought your dad was an
asshole. You thought most of your family and your
friends were racist sexist creeps. So you're different,
right. You're not a racist or a sexist. You just think
it's all shit. But how would it sound on tape.

JIMMY

It'd sound like you were listening to anyone who'd
been doing my job for ten years. Trying to separate
the real thing from all the pathetic whining.

JUDY

I think it'd sound like someone who was no longer
fit to do your job.

JIMMY

Hey. Some guy comes in and tells me he got fired
because of the colour of his skin and I find proof

he's right, I try to get that company fined out of
existence. But if a guy comes in and tells me I don't
understand what he's going through because I'm
not the same colour, I'm not "of" his religion, I
don't live where he lives, I groan real loud and tell
him not to waste my fucking time.

JUDY

But it sounds ugly, Jimmy. These days it sounds like
you just don't like a lot of people and the things
they believe in. And you just don't like them in a
very deep and disturbing way.

JIMMY

Sid, a.k.a. David, said I was making it difficult for
you to return to "your people." Forgetting for a
minute how offensive the term "your people" is,
what the hell was he talking about

JUDY

He knows how you feel about religion. So when I
go to shul he knows it's ... difficult. He's maybe
suggesting you make it less difficult for me.

JIMMY

Well ... you know ... fuck it. I mean is it a
coincidence that our marriage has been pretty
shaky since you started joining your family at
synagogue about a year ago.

JUDY

No. It was shaky before. That's one of the reasons I
started going.

JIMMY

Oh yeah and that's because your religion is
particularly insightful about modern marriage.

JUDY

No it's because I was lonely, Jimmy.

JIMMY
Lonely? Oh gimme a break. Whatya mean you were lonely.

JUDY
Let's go. We'll talk at home.

JIMMY
No. I don't like it there.

JUDY
Your children are there.

JIMMY
Bring them here. It's better here. That house is the place their parents' marriage is dissolving. There's the smell of rot in the air. It's emotionally unsafe in that house. The kids shouldn't be there.

JUDY
They like the house, Jimmy.

JIMMY
No take them away from it. Take them to your parents.

JUDY
What is this. You want me to leave you?

JIMMY
Yeah. I do.

JUDY
Why.

JIMMY
Because you want to. Because you're "lonely."

JUDY
What. You find that hard to believe? Well where's the man I married. The man who seemed so supportive and yeah "nice." He's gone. He's been replaced by a very difficult guy to live with. You

know what a big part of my problem is. I think you
probably have the same contempt for me you have
for almost everything else.

JIMMY

Well that's just not true.

JUDY

You think my work is a joke.

JIMMY

No. I don't. Not really.

JUDY

That's okay. Maybe it is. I mean maybe I'm just
doing these little films to avoid something. You
know, just keeping busy so I won't—

JIMMY

Please. You think you're great. You think your work
is great. You think you make a spectacular
difference.

JUDY

Look. If that's what I thought that's what I'd
fucking say. Try to listen to me for ten seconds. Hey
maybe that's your problem. Maybe you've stopped
paying attention. You're so eager to spew out your
answers you don't actually hear the questions.

JIMMY

What the hell does that mean.

JUDY

Well you've got all this power over people. And so
when you talk they have to—

JIMMY

I'm a government lawyer, Judy. I'm a fucking
dickless wonder.

JUDY

Who doesn't listen.

JIMMY

Jesus.

JUDY

But I remember when you did. And to a whole lot
of people, me included but immigrants mostly, you
were some kind of hero. You helped those people
when they couldn't get help anywhere else.

JIMMY

Yeah well ... fuck them.

JUDY

Fuck them? Why, Jimmy. How did we get to fuck
them.

JIMMY

Mostly because of what they bring with them. Their
tribal conflicts. So fuck the Vietnamese-hating
Cambodians. And the Cambodian-hating Koreans.
And the Jamaican-hating Trinidadians. And the
Albanian-hating Serbs ... hating Croats and
whoever else ... and yes while we're at it, Jude, fuck
the white European male and everyone he hates.
And all the Christian-hating Muslims and
Muslim-hating Jews and Jew-hating Christians and
gay-hating Christians and Muslim-hating Christians.
And black and white and yellow and red and so on
and so on. Fuck and double fuck them all. And if it
disappoints you that I feel that way well ... fuck you
too I guess.

Pause.

JUDY

Yeah well when you put it that way ... Actually I
hope you rot in hell for putting it that way, Jimmy.

JIMMY

And speaking of hell ...

JUDY

You mean our marriage?

JIMMY

And me not being the man you thought I was.
So ... your return to Judaism is really meant to do
what? Are you treating the synagogue as a singles
club, Judy. Are you looking for a nice Jewish guy to
replace me with.

JUDY

Whatya mean.

JIMMY

I mean are you looking for a boyfriend.

JUDY

I ... how do you ... what do you ... do you ...

JIMMY just looks at her. JUDY looks away.
DAVID comes back on.

DAVID

I had to come back. There's something wrong with
how I left.

JIMMY

You came back so you could leave better?

DAVID

I came back to explore the truth. No that's not
right. I don't want to *explore* the truth. I want to
actually *deal* with the truth.

JIMMY

Good for you, Sid. The truth about what.

JUDY

David, I don't think this is the best time for—

DAVID

    I can't do this. I thought for awhile I could. But I can't. I just can't.

JIMMY

    Well … don't.

JUDY

    Stay out of this, Jimmy.

JIMMY

    Stay out of what.

JUDY

    This is between me and David.

JIMMY

    What is.

DAVID

    Well obviously it concerns him too.

JIMMY

    What does?

DAVID

    James, I'm in love with your wife.

JIMMY

    I'm sorry?

DAVID

    If she divorces you I intend to marry her.

JIMMY

    Excuse me. (*goes to JUDY*) Is there something wrong with him.

JUDY

    What do you mean by that. He says he's in love with me and the first thing that occurs to you is maybe there's something wrong with him. Maybe he's just fine. Maybe he just loves me.

JIMMY

Uh huh. But ... so what. So what if he loves you.
I'm sure lots of men love you. I mean why is he
telling me he loves you. The only reason for telling
me that he loves you is if you love him too.

DAVID

She does.

JIMMY

Do you.

DAVID

She does.

JIMMY

You do, don't you.

JUDY

I ... don't know.

DAVID

She knows. (*to JUDY*) Why are you saying you don't
know.

JUDY

I don't know.

JIMMY

Judy ... What is this. You love this guy? You love
your rabbi? Is that allowed. Holy shit I was right.
You've been man-hunting.

JUDY

No. It just happened.

DAVID

Nothing happened. We just love each other ... But
nothing ... happened. I just felt bad about
counselling you on your marriage James, so I came
back to tell you that I have these feelings for Judy
and to absolve myself of any hypocrisy I might have

61

engaged in. So I've done that. And I feel better. And also now you know about us and I feel better about that too. And so now ... I have to leave.

DAVID leaves.
Pause.

JUDY

I have to leave too.

JUDY leaves. In the same direction as DAVID.
Pause.

JIMMY

(*yelling after her*) I had a fucking heart attack six weeks ago! I almost fucking died! Thanks for all your fucking compassion!!

He stands. And kicks his wheelchair to death.
Blackout.

Scene Four

KARL and DEREK are fighting. DEREK punches KARL.
KARL gets him in a bear hug and throws him down.

KARL

You piece of shit. Who's the piece of shit here.
Here's a clue. It's not me! You piece of shit.
Fucking with me like that. Fucking with me like I'm
a piece of shit. Never ever fucking try that again.
You hear me, piece of shit? You hear me?

KARL kneels beside DEREK. Yanks his head up by the
hair.

KARL

Do you hear me?!

DEREK

Yeah.

KARL

Do you hear me and understand me?!

DEREK

Yeah.

KARL

Do you really. Do you?!

DEREK

Yeah. Yeah I really do.

KARL

Yeah? So who's a piece of shit.

DEREK

I am.

KARL

And who *isn't* a piece of shit.

DEREK

You.

KARL

So how long are you gonna keep fucking with me.
I've given you money. I've given you time. I've
given you a second chance. A third chance. But do
I have that gun. No.

DEREK

The guy moved. He changed location. I've been
trying to find him.

KARL

For weeks. For weeks you've been trying to find
him. You know something. That sounds like a lie.
Are you gonna admit right now that it's a lie or am
I gonna have to kill you!

DEREK

It's a lie.

KARL

And is it the last lie I'm ever gonna hear from you.

DEREK

Yes! Yes it is.

KARL

Because who will never ever lie to me again or fuck
with me again. Say it!

DEREK

I will never ...

KARL

Never *ever.*

DEREK

Never ever fuck with you again.

KARL

Because?

DEREK

Because I'm a piece of shit—

KARL

And I'm?

DEREK

Not a piece of shit.

KARL sees JUDY approaching. She stops and watches.

KARL

Good. Now get up. Come on. On your feet.

He helps DEREK up.

KARL

Straighten yourself up. You look like crap. Good.
Now fuck off outta here. You've only got an hour to
do what you gotta do, man. You need to be back
here in one hour exactly or I'm coming after you.
With malicious intent.

DEREK

Yeah okay.

KARL

Bye.

DEREK starts off.

KARL

Hey wait. Got a smoke?

DEREK

Yeah.

*DEREK takes out a pack. Starts to pull a cigarette
from the pack.*

KARL

Hey whatya doin'? Don't fucking take one out. Just leave me the pack. What. Are we gonna be fucking stingy with each other now.

DEREK hands him the pack.

KARL

Thanks.

DEREK

Yeah.

DEREK leaves with a bit of difficulty. Holding his side.
KARL sits down on the picnic table. Lights up.
Inhales.
JUDY approaches slowly.

JUDY

You know something Karl? When Jimmy first introduced us, I thought you were just an irritating prick. Now I find out you're one of the most evil people on the planet.

KARL

What were you doing. Just standing there, Jude?

JUDY

Yeah. Listening. Thinking. Getting a bit sick to my stomach.

KARL

It's just job stuff, Judy. I need that kid to be afraid of me. Nothing productive happens between us if he isn't afraid ... It's just an act.

JUDY

Maybe the act is you pretending to be a human being when you're really a demented monster.

KARL

So you spend a lot of time walking alone at night in parks these days Judy.

JUDY

I was looking for Jimmy.

KARL

Yeah? I heard about his heart. How is he anyway.

JUDY

Great. Totally recovered. It's like there was never anything wrong with him. Doctors can't explain it. I think it's his anger. He's so fucking angry it's making him impervious to disease.

KARL

What's he got to be angry about. Cushy job. Cushy home. Cushy wife ... Want a smoke?

JUDY

I don't smoke.

KARL

Of course you don't ... Come on over here. Sit down. It's been years since we talked.

JUDY

We've talked?

KARL

Well ... let's talk now.

JUDY

Whatya doing to that kid.

KARL

You want to talk about that?

JUDY

What's that stuff about a gun all about.

KARL

You heard that? How long were you out there.

JUDY

Long enough. So? About the gun.

KARL

Come on over here and I'll tell you about it.

JUDY

I'm okay here.

KARL

You still making those documentaries?

JUDY

Yeah.

KARL

I saw that one you made about homeless mothers
and their kids. I cried.

JUDY

Sure you did.

KARL

No I did. I was ashamed of it at the time. But I've
become emotionally unblocked since then.
Anyway ... this could be a documentary. This story
about me and the kid and the gun. You wanna
hear it?

JUDY

Maybe.

KARL

Come on over. Sit down. Let's get cozy.

JUDY

Yeah right. Cozy.

She starts over slowly.

KARL

I mean it's a long story. And well it's not ... pretty.
So I don't want innocent passersby to have to listen
to it.

JUDY

(*sitting*) You're a sensitive guy, Karl.

KARL

No I'm a monster. Remember?

JUDY

Yeah. So what's the story.

KARL

It's a story about a monster. Once upon a time—no
let's skip all that and get to the good part. This is it.
This is the good part. You die. (*He grabs her throat
with one hand. Squeezes. Puts his other arm across her
chest. Pins her to the bench.*) You die and your dear
husband gets to feel how I felt when he killed my
partner. I guess it's a story about fate. I mean I
guess you thought your fate was to accidentally
stumble across me behaving in a monster-like way
with a young and probably deeply abused and
misunderstood member of the criminal class and
then taking that information to your husband so he
could fuck me over in that way he has of fucking
cops over who are just doing their job. But that
wasn't your fate was it. Dead yet? Dead yet, Judy?
You know it's too bad it turned out like this
because—No that's wrong. It's okay that it turned
out like this. I mean look around. Things are
turning out like this more or less in a lot of places.
I mean what's happened. What's happened to our
beloved city. To the world. Hey. What's happened
to me. I mean I wasn't always a monster. Even you

69

gotta admit that. I mean some people even thought I had a certain amount of charm. Dead yet? ... Yeah? ... Okay.

He lets her go.
She falls off the bench.
He gets up and walks away.
Blackout.

Scene Five

SISSY on stilts. Crosses slowly at the back of the park.
Holding on to trees ... whatever.
JIMMY and DAVID sit some distance apart. DAVID is
watching SISSY. JIMMY has his head bowed. They are
both wearing dark suits that are quite crumpled.
JIMMY's shirt is open at the collar. DAVID has a rose in
his lapel. They sit silently awhile. Lost in thought.

DAVID

James ... (*no response*) ... James ...

JIMMY slowly lifts his head, looks at DAVID for a
moment.

JIMMY

What.

DAVID

(*pointing to SISSY*) What's that all about.

JIMMY

She's ... trying to better herself.

DAVID

How is this bettering herself.

JIMMY

A few weeks ago she was begging on the street.

SISSY has moved out of sight.

DAVID

Why doesn't she just get a job.

JIMMY

She can't get a job. She doesn't live anywhere. No
one hires people who don't live anywhere.

71

DAVID

Do you think she takes drugs.

JIMMY

Yes. I do.

DAVID

This is a sad place. You brought your family to live in a sad and dangerous part of the city, James.

JIMMY

The kids were excited about moving downtown.

DAVID

What about Judy.

JIMMY

It was her idea.

DAVID

Really. Why'd I think it was yours.

JIMMY

I don't know. I don't know why you think any of the things you do, Sid. Why'd you think that stupid rose was an appropriate thing to wear to a funeral.

DAVID

I wore it for Judy. She liked roses.

JIMMY

No she didn't ... Did she?

DAVID

Yes. She liked them a lot.

JIMMY

Well fuck you for knowing that.

Pause.

JIMMY

Anyway it's dead. You can take it off now.

DAVID
I don't want to.

JIMMY
And you can stop wearing that suit. It's been almost
two weeks.

DAVID
I'll stop wearing mine when you stop wearing yours.

JIMMY
You can't turn this into a contest about who loved
her more. Just change your fucking suit. You're
starting to smell.

DAVID
You should talk.

    Pause.

JIMMY
Ah man. What am I gonna do without her.

DAVID
I don't know.

    SISSY crosses back across the park.

JIMMY
I wasn't really looking for an answer from you
there.

    Pause.

DAVID
How long is she going to keep doing that.

JIMMY
She's just gaining confidence.

DAVID
She doesn't look like she's gaining confidence.

JIMMY

She doesn't have to "look" like she's gaining it. She just has to gain it.

SISSY is out of sight.
DAVID lowers his head.

DAVID

Do you think the children will be all right.

JIMMY

No.

DAVID

I think they'll be all right eventually.

JIMMY

Their mother was murdered. They're never going to be all right.

DAVID

Maybe they should spend some time with their grandparents. I mean Judy's parents.

JIMMY

No kidding ... I didn't think you were suggesting I send them to live with that barbarian bitch I call *my* mother.

DAVID

Calm down, Jimmy. I was just—

JIMMY

First of all don't ever tell me to calm down. Next never call me Jimmy. And finally I know what you're trying to do, you prick. You want my kids in your temple. And you think Judy's parents will deliver them to you.

DAVID

The community can help them at a time like this.

JIMMY

No one can help them at a time like this. Their mother was murdered! Goddamnit! They're fucked forever, don't you know that!

DAVID

I'm sorry. I shouldn't have—

JIMMY

No. God that was ... I didn't mean that. I'm just so—

DAVID

It's my fault. I shouldn't be advising you right now. I'm not thinking clearly because how I felt about her is making me—

JIMMY

Look ... you can have the kids. Take them to Judy's mom and dad. Take them ... to their people. Do whatever you can to help them, okay? Maybe with help they could survive this.

DAVID

So could you.

JIMMY

Shut up about me, okay?

SISSY appears on the stilts again.

SISSY

Hey! Look! No hands!

JIMMY

Great!

SISSY crosses out of sight.
DAVID is up. Looking around.

DAVID

Do you think it was a hate crime, Jimmy. Judy's
murder. There are lots of blacks around here. A lot
of them hate Jews, you know.

JIMMY

Ah don't do this.

DAVID

But it could have been a hate crime.

JIMMY

And it probably was. But against women. Not Jews.

DAVID

You don't know that for sure. I can't assume that.

JIMMY

What's that mean. You "can't assume that." You
planning to take some action here? You planning
to call in the Mossad? Maybe do a little ethnic
cleansing of the area?

DAVID

Listen, I'm just saying—

JIMMY

You're a racist, aren't you.

DAVID

No I'm not.

JIMMY

Come on. Admit it. There's no one around. If you
admit it, you'll feel better. That's what I was always
taught. You're a racist.

DAVID

No. You're a racist. I'm a Jew.

JIMMY

You lost me there Sid.

DAVID
>
> People who have been victimized in the way we have can't possibly be considered—

JIMMY
>
> Some of the biggest racists I ever met in my fucking life were Jews.

DAVID
>
> Excluding every single Christian on the planet you mean!

JIMMY
>
> Yeah. Right. That's what I mean ... Look shut up. I'm in mourning here.

DAVID
>
> So am I, Jimmy. So am I. I loved her too.

JIMMY
>
> Yeah ... How insensitive of me to forget that.

> *SISSY comes on.*

SISSY
>
> Hey! Look at this!

> *She does a pose or a trick on the stilts.*

JIMMY
>
> Great!

SISSY
>
> Wanna try it?

JIMMY
>
> Maybe later.

> *SISSY turns and leaves.*

DAVID
>
> All right I *am* a racist. I don't like blacks.

JIMMY
>
> But I suppose you've got a good reason for that.

DAVID

They're violent.

JIMMY

All of them?

DAVID

Too many of them.

JIMMY

And that has nothing to do with being largely
excluded from a white man's world.

DAVID

I was talking as a man. I was being bluntly honest. I
was admitting weakness. I know there are all sorts
of reasons why people behave in certain ways. I'm
an educated person. Man to man. I'm a racist. I
shouldn't be. I mean I'm a Jew and Jews—

JIMMY

Yeah, yeah. Jews are blah blah. Hey Sid. You're not
just a Jew. You're a rabbi. And you don't dislike just
blacks. I've caught your act a couple of times.
You're not big on Arabs either.

DAVID

Yes well that's war, James. They're my enemy.

JIMMY

You're a goddamn rabbi. You shouldn't have any
enemies.

DAVID

What ever gave you that idea. There's nothing in
my faith that says you have to let yourself be
destroyed. That you can't strike back if you—

JIMMY

Maybe you need counselling.

DAVID

What kind of counselling.

JIMMY

Career counselling. Maybe you're not cut out for
this line of work. Maybe you're just too ... human.

DAVID

What's that mean.

JIMMY

It's a really human thing. To need someone to kick.
Especially if you've been kicked a lot yourself.

DAVID

I don't need to kick anyone. I was talking about
protecting the borders of a country. Scud missiles,
terrorist attacks, indiscriminate bombings of—

JIMMY

I saw this black kid and he was—

DAVID

What black kid.

JIMMY

This black kid yelling at another kid in a school
yard a couple months ago. The black kid was
yelling "Go home you fucking Paki." And guess
what the other kid yells back "I'm not a Paki. I'm
from India." And I thought oh great, they're gonna
form a bond. The black kid and the kid from India
have got something in common now. Neither of
them is a Paki. So they can get together and go out
and find themselves one. And kick the poor little
bastard to death ... Ah fuck it. I give up. Everybody
hates everybody ... Okay let's just go with that and
see where it takes us.

SISSY is walking across the park. Juggling.

DAVID
  Look. She's juggling.

JIMMY
  Yeah.

DAVID
  That's amazing.

JIMMY
  Yeah ...

DAVID
  And she does all that on drugs. I marvel at people's capacity.

JIMMY
  Do you. Do you "marvel" Sid.

DAVID
  Don't you think that under the circumstances ... our mutual grief ... you could use my real name.

JIMMY
  Which is?

DAVID
  I mean I don't really get it. Why Sid? Is it supposed to be an ethnic slur. What's wrong with the name Sid anyway.

JIMMY
  You're the one who's got the problem with it.

DAVID
  Call me David. Please. I'm asking nicely. I know you're not really an anti-Semite. You're just a very disappointed man. I know that ... well basically ... you're disappointed in everyone. Judy told me how much you hate the Catholic church so I know it's not just a Jew thing ... So ...

JIMMY
So ... what.

DAVID
So why not call me David.

JIMMY
Speaking of Pakies ... the Islamic faith. There are
some pretty zany guys hiding out in that religion.
The Taliban ... How many women can you kill in
the name of Allah. What's the record so far. Those
thugs should be dragged into the new millennium
no matter how much they kick and scream. You
know what Einstein called the big three, the
Christian, Jewish, Islamic faiths. The religions of
fear. They all gotta go. Really ... We can't get
anywhere holding on to them. They're anti-
evolutionary ... I used to say that to Judy ... How
can you be part of a faith that doesn't like you.

DAVID
That's blatantly untrue.

JIMMY
"Back of the temple, bitch" ... Like my mother. And
my sisters. Good Catholics ... But their church
despises them. On some fundamental level. It does.

DAVID
I ... think ... I'll go back and cook the children
supper.

JIMMY
Pardon.

DAVID
They're alone. They haven't eaten.

JIMMY
So you're going to cook them supper.

DAVID

I've been cooking meals for them for several days, James. Are you going to tell me now that you object.

JIMMY

No … I was just … No I appreciate what you're doing. I think it's nice.

DAVID

Okay then. (*he starts off*)

JIMMY

Hey.

> *DAVID stops.*

JIMMY

Jealousy. I'm pretty sure it was jealousy that made me start calling you Sid.

DAVID

What. You knew how Judy and I felt about each other?

JIMMY

No. It wasn't that. It was the "our people" thing. It's like a club. She belonged. You belonged. I couldn't join.

DAVID

You could have converted.

JIMMY

Oh yeah that would have worked.

DAVID

Well it's not meant to be a club, Jimmy.

JIMMY

Well that's what it seems like. If you're married to a person who—well anyway from the outside it looks like an exclusive club. It's just … rude.

DAVID

Rude?

JIMMY

Yeah, David. It's fucking rude to belong to
something that excludes people.

DAVID

You called me David.

JIMMY

So what.

DAVID

Thank you. That means a lot to me.

He starts off.

JIMMY

Oh right. Make a big deal of it.

*DAVID meets up with SISSY who is heading in his
direction.*

DAVID

You're very good.

SISSY

Getting there ... Look, can you do me a favour. I'm
gonna try to make it to the street. Maybe get some
money in the hat from a few pedestrians. You got a
hat?

DAVID

No.

SISSY

Well we'll find something. Think you could walk
alongside me? Just in case I ... you know ... fall.

DAVID

Sure.

SISSY

Thanks.

They start off.

DAVID

Maybe you could join a circus.

SISSY

What.

DAVID

They hire people like you.

SISSY

What's that mean. People like me.

DAVID

Well people on stilts ... who can juggle. I mean you could actually get a job with those skills.

SISSY

I was thinking I'd just sort of do it on the street or something.

They are on their way.

DAVID

But if you had a job ... I mean if you did it full time there'd be benefits. You know dental care, a pension plan.

SISSY

I don't know really know what you're talking about.

DAVID

It's just something to consider. How old are you.

SISSY

How old are you.

DAVID

I'm thirty-eight.

SISSY

I'm sixteen ... Ah no ... no yeah I'm still sixteen.

They are gone.

JIMMY lowers his head.

The lights change.

In the distance but getting closer real fast, the sound of a helicopter accompanied by some Wagner ... Suddenly the air is filled with a thumping disco beat like they play at NBA games and an announcer bellows.

ANNOUNCER

Ladies! And gentlemen! Are you ready!?

The recorded crowd responds in the affirmative.

ANNOUNCER

Then let's get ready to rumble!!!

And now the helicopter is right overhead. Stirring up the ground below and JUDY is lowered down by a rope or cable ... or ... She is wearing commando gear. With a few designer flourishes. She hits the ground, unhooks herself, does a few fancy martial arts moves. And then turns to JIMMY.

JUDY

Okay asshole. Get ready. It's payback time.

JIMMY looks up. Wide-eyed.

JIMMY

Holy fuck.

JUDY

You said it.

She spins and kicks him in the head.

JUDY

Okay. Here's the deal about heaven. First, it's true that you can be anything you want. I thought being a member of some kind of killer elite would be satisfying. So far so good. Also it's easy to get to heaven because all you gotta do is believe in it. You see heaven's a place only for people who need it I guess. Which brings us to my problem. Apparently the heaven I believed in was a Christian heaven. Just another example of how you co-opted my whole life you rotten bastard.

She hits him with a left and a right then jumps and kicks him in the chest. He falls back over the bench.

JUDY

Man. That felt good. Like my outfit? I designed it myself. I'm an awesome designer. And remember how I wasn't great at math. Ask me something. Ask me long division. Pick any twelve digit number and let me divide it by anything you want. No? ... Well maybe later. Anyway you never answered. Do you like my outfit? It's meant to intimidate and yet at the same time subtly seduce. As in, "I'm gonna kill ya but you're gonna love it." I'm never taking it off. Clothing is optional in heaven but I'm already pretty tired of all those Franciscans staring at my ass. I mean even in heaven that's still a real problem. Guys who just didn't get enough. You know, priests, construction workers, government consultants. They all need to be watched real close. ... Anyway I hope you're happy ... I'm in Christian heaven. The Franciscans are staring at my ass. And everyone's quoting the New Testament like it's a best seller or something. Oh yeah and the thing I always thought about those fundamentalist preachers was right on. They're just mean pricks. Even in heaven. Mean self-righteous pricks. Some angel or someone says to them "Hey you don't have to be like that. It's heaven. You can be anything you want." And they say "We wanna be like this. Bless the Lord. Heal." (*she lays a hand on his forehead. He falls back*) Look I think you should be with the kids ... Don't let other people take care of them, cook for them, comfort them ... What's wrong with you anyway ... Be a man about this whole thing. Get on with it. Take care of your children.

JIMMY

I miss you.

JUDY

I miss you too.

JIMMY

I ... love you ... and I ... I can't ...

JUDY

It's okay. Just take a deep breath.

He does.

JIMMY

I can't ... shake this feeling that I'm somehow responsible for what happened to you. Who killed you.

JUDY

I can't tell you.

JIMMY

Why not.

JUDY

Well there are two possible reasons. One. I could be a figment of your imagination. And if you don't know how would I.

JIMMY

What's the other reason.

JUDY

Well why do you need to know. So you can take
revenge? Yeah that'd be great. Wind up in prison.
Or get yourself killed. Here's the thing Jimmy.
You're gonna be called upon soon. You're gonna
have to stand up for something. Do a little battling
for something you believe in. It's not gonna be
good enough to be against everything Jimmy.
You're gonna have to be *for* something. Get ready
for it. It's gonna happen soon.

JIMMY

What's gonna happen soon.

JUDY

What I just told you. Christ even when I'm dead
you don't listen to me.

JIMMY

But I don't understand. This battle thing. What is
it.

JUDY

You know. Deep down you probably know. Kiss the
kids for me.

> *A wind starts to blow.*
> *JUDY throws her head back. Holds out her arms.*
> *The helicopter can be heard returning.*
> *The wind is coming from all directions and is getting*
> *very fierce.*

JUDY

Gotta go ... Hold on to something.

> *JIMMY holds on to a tree or a bench.*
> *The rope is lowered from the helicopter.*
> *JUDY struggles to it ... and hooks herself up.*

JIMMY
    Wait.

JUDY
    No.

JIMMY
    Why not.

JUDY
    Don't want to.

> *JUDY gets pulled up and away ... The helicopter flies off ... JIMMY is now being blown around the park ... Slowly the wind subsides.*
> *JIMMY sits.*
> *Blackout.*

Scene Six

Night.
KARL, DEREK, and SISSY.
*SISSY is on the ground unconscious. DEREK is trying
to wake her up. KARL is pacing. Waving an
automatic pistol and gesturing.*

DEREK

Come on girl. Come on wake up.

KARL

You better wake her up.

DEREK

I'm trying to wake her up.

KARL

You better fucking wake her up.

DEREK

Wake up, girl!

KARL

I'll hurt you bad. I mean it. I need to see that girl
awake and talking. And if I don't see that pretty
soon I'm gonna hurt you. It's that simple.

DEREK

Wake up, girl! (*shaking her*) Just wake up okay?

KARL

What did you give her.

DEREK

I didn't give her nothin'.

> *KARL cuffs DEREK on the back of the head.*

KARL

What did you give her.

DEREK

Her usual.

KARL

And what the fuck's that.

DEREK

A bit of this. That. You know. Shit.

KARL

You don't remember, do you. You don't care. It
could be three parts Drano and you wouldn't
fucking care.

DEREK

No no that's not true. I—

KARL

Hey don't argue with me about this stuff. Haven't
we already agreed that you're a piece of shit ... All I
want you to do now is wake that girl up. I need to
know what she saw.

DEREK

I'm pretty sure she didn't see anything.

KARL

You're pretty sure? (*puts the gun to* DEREK*'s head*) Are
you pretty sure I've got this gun to your head. Or
are you absofuckinglutely sure. You see the
difference? You see how I need to be sure? Wake
her the fuck up.

DEREK

(*shaking her*) Wake the fuck up!

KARL

Why'd you take her there anyway. Are you an idiot.

DEREK

She wanted to come.

KARL

That's it? That's the reason you took her. Because she wanted to come.

DEREK

Basically.

KARL

You were goin' off to kill someone, you stupid little prick.

DEREK

I didn't plan for her to watch. I told her to stay back. But she'd already taken the shit so she was ... Anyway I didn't know you'd be there. You told me to do it.

KARL

Well why do you think I was there, Derek. Maybe because I thought you weren't up to it. Do you think maybe that's why I had to put myself in that position.

DEREK

Well it's not my fault you don't have any fucking faith in people.

KARL

Oh fuck off.

DEREK

I'm just saying you didn't need to be there. I was intending to do it.

KARL

You were intending to do it for one fucking long time, son. I was watching you from that guy's hallway for maybe ten minutes.

DEREK

Hey I got the gun from him, didn't I.

KARL

Yeah you got the gun. And you stood there with it
for ten minutes babbling and crying like a little kid.

DEREK

I was working up to it. If you hadn't stepped in I
would have done it. I know I would have done it. I
was just getting—

KARL

Look just shut up. And wake her up and ask her
what she saw. Wake her up!

DEREK

(*shaking SISSY*) Wake up, girl!

KARL

Hey. It's working. Her eyes opened there a bit.
Shake her.

DEREK

(*shaking her*) Wake up, Sissy. Sissy!

KARL

Look. Her eyes. Yeah. Okay.

DEREK

Good, Sissy. Open your eyes, girl. Open them up!
Good!

SISSY

What's ... up ...

DEREK

Everything's goin' good. Everything's just—

SISSY

I don't ... feel so great. What'd you give me.

DEREK

    Your usual.

SISSY

    No it was—

KARL

    Ask her!

DEREK

    Sissy when we were at the guy's house, what did you
    see happen.

SISSY

    What guy.

DEREK

    That guy ... at the house.

SISSY

    What house.

DEREK

    Don't you remember a house.

SISSY

    We were ... here ... You gave me something.

KARL

    You don't remember?

SISSY

    No ... I don't ... remember ...

      She passes out.

DEREK

    She's gone again.

KARL

    Yeah ... Put her down.

DEREK

    What.

KARL

   Put her head down.

DEREK

   Yeah, okay. (*does it*) But that's good. She doesn't
   remember. So that's—

KARL

   Give me a minute.

DEREK

   Sure. But we're clean, right? What the fuck do you
   want from me, man!

KARL

   She's clean.

DEREK

   Whatya mean.

KARL

   I wasn't fully committed to hurting her anyway.
   That would not really have been too cool a thing to
   do. I mean look at her. Hasn't she been hurt
   enough. Go ahead. Look at her. Look ... at ... her.
   Whatya see.

DEREK

   I don't—

KARL

   Garbage? I mean I look at her and I see garbage.
   Your garbage. So just outta curiosity is that what
   you see. Some sixteen-year-old got hooked on drugs
   and made into garbage.

DEREK

   But she was a druggie when I met her. I just—

KARL

   Fuck it. I don't really give a shit.

   He shoots DEREK. DEREK drops to his knees.

KARL

    I was just making an observation. The thing is she didn't see me kill that guy so she can live. You *did*. So you *can't*.

        KARL shoots DEREK in the face. DEREK falls over. Dead.

KARL

    Don't wake up, girl. If you wake up you have to die.

        He kicks her a little. She stays unconscious.

KARL

    Good for you.

        He puts the gun away.
        Sirens in the distance.
        Blackout.

Scene Seven

Early morning.
Police tape around the area where DEREK died. His
body is gone.
KARL sits on a bench. SISSY beside him. They sit
silently. KARL is patting her head.
JIMMY off to one side watching them. Pacing.
DAVID comes on. Sees JIMMY.

DAVID
Good.

> *He heads for JIMMY.*

DAVID
I need to talk to you. I'm worried about your
children.

> *JIMMY grabs him. Gestures toward KARL and SISSY.*

JIMMY
What is this.

DAVID
What's what.

JIMMY
There's something wrong with this picture. The
kindly undercover cop.

DAVID
He's a policeman? He looks like a vagrant.

JIMMY
Can you do me a favour.

DAVID
I'm worried about your children. They've asked me
to talk to you about—

JIMMY

 Sure. Okay. But in the meantime can you do me a
 favour.

DAVID

 They just want you to spend some time with them.
 They don't understand why you're so remote.

JIMMY

 I want you to take Sissy to my house.

DAVID

 Sissy. Who's Sissy?

JIMMY

 That's Sissy. I want you to take her home. Introduce
 her to the kids. Make her something to eat.

DAVID

 Why.

JIMMY

 You're a good cook. Since Judy was killed, all the
 meals you've made, maybe a few dozen meals ...
 and there wasn't a dud amongst them.

DAVID

 Thank you ... I feel it's the least I can do.

JIMMY

 It probably is. Come on.

   JIMMY leads DAVID over toward KARL and SISSY.

JIMMY

 You finished with her, Karl?

KARL

 Hi, Jimmy. You hear about what went down here
 earlier?

JIMMY

 Yeah ... You finished with her?

KARL

    Her friend and mentor was killed. Black kid. Derek.
Maybe you'd seen him around.

JIMMY

    Did she see how it happened.

KARL

    No.

JIMMY

    So she can go?

KARL

    Sure she can go. She's got nowhere to go to. But if
she did, she could go there. No fucking problem.

JIMMY

    You want a place to crash, Sissy?

SISSY

    You got a place ?

JIMMY

    Yeah ... Sid, David will take you there. You
remember him?

SISSY

    Yeah. From before. Hi Sid. (*stands slowly, puts her
hand out*)

DAVID

    David.

        He takes her hand.

SISSY

    Yeah. Sid David? Right?

DAVID

    No. Just David ... Come on, it's just down the street.

        They start off. DAVID is more or less holding her up.

KARL
    Bye, sweetheart.

DAVID
    Are you all right.

SISSY
    Derek's dead.

DAVID
    I know.

SISSY
    I'm pretty fucked up about it ... He was my friend.

DAVID
    I'm sorry.

       They are gone.

KARL
    Who's the guy.

JIMMY
    Judy's rabbi. He's helping me with the kids.

KARL
    How are they.

JIMMY
    I ... don't know. Not great.

KARL
    I'm sorry about Judy. Did you get my card.

JIMMY
    No.

KARL
    I sent you a card.

JIMMY
    I didn't get it.

KARL

I'm not lying, man. I sent you a fucking card. I can
even describe it. It was yellow. On the front it said
"Sorry for your loss." On the inside it said
"Thinking of you." I signed it "Karl, your childhood
friend" and I added "let bygones be bygones." Ring
any bells?

JIMMY

No.

KARL

Well I sent it.

JIMMY

Are you on anything, Karl.

KARL

Amphetamines. Maintenance dose. Well I work all
these strange hours. Are you asking me because
you're concerned about my health.

JIMMY

No. I'm asking because you're talking like a fucking
lunatic.

KARL

(*laughs*) Yeah. Right. Same old Jimmy.

JIMMY

Were you around when the kid got killed.

KARL

Well I was in the vicinity.

JIMMY

Whatya think happened.

KARL

Someone shot him. He died.

JIMMY

And that's it?

KARL

Isn't that enough. (*laughs*) That's definitely it as far as I'm concerned, buddy. He was not one of God's better creations. Oh was that harsh. Was he a friend of yours or something. Someone you cared about. Someone you thought you could help overcome his unfortunate circumstances.

JIMMY

Okay. Well it's been a blast ...

JIMMY starts off.

KARL

Where you goin'.

JIMMY

Home.

KARL

Who said you could leave.

JIMMY

(*stops*) What.

KARL

I'm still talkin' to you. (*approaches JIMMY*) I mean a murder took place her earlier. I'm a police officer. And you're a local resident. And I might need to ask you what you saw or heard or something like that. The point is you can't fucking go anywhere until I say you can.

JIMMY looks at him awhile.

JIMMY

Okay.

KARL

So ... How's your agony.

JIMMY

My what.

KARL

Your agony. Is it fully formed yet. Does it have a
personality. Does it come and go when you least
expect it. Does it get into bed with you. Does it
whisper to you. Does it crawl inside your brain ...
So how is it.

JIMMY

It's there.

KARL

So ... You and Judy. No one ever thought it was one
of those made-for-each-other relationships. But
from what I hear it got downright ugly near the
end there. You must have mixed feelings about her
untimely demise ... Come on, admit it. Don't you
ever feel like you've been presented with an
opportunity to meet someone else, get it right ...
It wasn't that she was a Jew. It's just that she was
middle class. It's the class thing more than the
religion thing ... I mean basically you're white trash
... I mean your mother went to church a lot but
basically she was a whore, right ... Well?

JIMMY

Can I go now.

KARL

You don't wanna go. You wanna stay and kick the
shit outta me. Admit it.

JIMMY

Why do I think you were involved in that kid's
death somehow.

KARL

Beats me.

JIMMY

Were you.

KARL

Suppose I said yeah. What would you do. Come
after me. You and your buddies in the government.
Expose me. Humiliate me. Fire me. Put me on trial.
Jail me.

JIMMY

Were you involved.

KARL

You fucking pussy. "Were you involved." What kind
of a fucking question is that. Ask a man's question.
Ask me if I killed the little scum bucket.

JIMMY

Did you.

KARL

Yeah. (*pulls out his gun*) With this. Same gun I killed
Ramon Alonzo with. Ramon Alonzo for your
information was a priest. From Nicaragua. A priest
who loved the children of the street. Who loved
them and kept them safe from the evils of the
world. All of the evils. Except himself. Now don't
get me wrong. I didn't kill Ramon Alonzo because
he fucked little boys. I killed him because he owed
me money. But that's a long story. Here's a shorter
one. I lost this gun. It somehow got taken from me
by a lowlife whore I thought was my soulmate.
Then it fell into the hands of her pimp. And I've
been to hell and back trying to retrieve it from the
rancid cocksucker ever since. I mean Jesus this gun
is a priest killer. A ballistics test on this could fuck
me up forever. Because it's my official gun. It's got
my name on it if you know what I mean. So ... all
you gotta do is get this gun from me and I'm
finished. You've won. Another cop bites the dust.

Jimmy does it again. So. Want to take it from me?
Wanna try?

JIMMY
   Maybe later.

   JIMMY starts off.

KARL
   Don't you wanna know what I did without a gun all
   that time.

JIMMY
   Not really.

KARL
   What I did to dispense justice. To put things right
   ... I called upon my inner strength. Gee now I'm
   talking like a pussy. "Inner strength." What the
   fuck's that. I just strangled people.

   JIMMY stops.

KARL
   What happened there, Jimmy. A little electric shock
   right up your spine.

   JIMMY turns back. Looks at KARL.

KARL
   Well aren't you going to say anything. I practically
   confessed to killing your wife, asshole. And you're
   not going to make a comment about that. Or do
   anything about that ... Are you just gonna stand
   there and feel ... bad.

   Pause.

JIMMY
   Why?

KARL
   She pissed me off.

Pause.

JIMMY

How'd she do that, Karl.

KARL

Hey I can't fucking remember now. That was like
weeks ago. I've killed several people since then ...
Oh yeah that's right. I'm outta control. I'm
seriously fucking gone ... Anyway about Judy, I
don't really think she pissed me off that much. I
think I killed her to get to you. And also I guess I
killed her ... because I could. I'm into that. That
doing it because I can thing. That's fucked, eh.
Yeah. Seriously ... Anyway. What are you going to
do about it ... You wanna do something about it?
Or are you just gonna stand there in shock ... Oh
my you must be feeling really bad. A part of me
shares your pain. Okay I gotta go ... There's
hundreds of people out there who need a little
dispensement of justice. Before I go ... Wanna hug?
... No. Okay ... Whatever ... (*leaving*) Anyway,
Jimmy. If you wanna take me down you're gonna
have to do it in a very personal way. I've covered my
trail. Nothing can be proved. So if you want me to
be accountable it's up to you, babe. (*laughs*)

KARL is gone.
JIMMY collapses on to his knees. Then lowers his head.
Sobbing.
Blackout.

Scene Eight

A slightly different kind of lighting. Maybe a starry night.
JIMMY alone. JUDY suddenly appears in a spotlight.
JUDY is dressed as a surgeon, in an operating gown, gloves, etc. She appears to be waiting.
JIMMY is just staring at her. Trying to figure out what's going on.

JUDY

Of course no one is ever really sick. But they let me operate on them anyway. You know just pretend. Because well ... they're kind ... And they know I wanted to be a doctor ever since I was seven. And you know the only reason I never became a doctor? Because my mother pissed me off by telling me I should be a nurse. So that I could meet a doctor marry him and have kids. Of course then I'd have to quit work period. But at least all that extra education that a doctor needs wouldn't have been wasted ... on me.

The loud sounds of a Formula One Grand Prix race ... Cars roaring ... then suddenly the sounds of a horrific crash.

JUDY

Here comes my patient now ... I'm particularly good at sports injuries.

DEREK falls down from above. Maybe if there is construction on one of the buildings at the edge of the park he can come down a chute into a dumpster.

DEREK climbs out of the dumpster. He is wearing a silver race car driver's safety suit.

DEREK

Wow. That was amazing.

JUDY

Derek, did you hurt yourself. Do you need anything fixed.

DEREK

I crashed into a safety wall. There was a horrible fiery explosion.

JUDY

(*to JIMMY*) Just pretend though.

DEREK

(*to JIMMY*) That's right. Just pretend. But it was exciting anyway.

JUDY

Did they stabilize you at the crash sight. Did they take your B.P. Did you get an M.R.I ... an E.K.G. Is everything A-Okay.

DEREK

You know what the best thing was? I could feel everyone in the stands was really worried about me. Thousands of people who all loved me and wanted me to live.

JIMMY

So I'm imagining you both, right. I'm trying to deal with this by ... what ... pretending you're all right. I mean I don't know what to do about Karl or feel about Karl, so I'm letting myself off the hook by ... what ... believing you're both ... what ... Better off?

JUDY

I'm in heaven.

DEREK
    So am I … I guess.

JIMMY
    So I'm supposed to … what, reassess my view of the
    world … or … what … I'm supposed to think that
    really … everything is … What. What am I
    supposed to think. That Karl is just the worst thing
    anyone can become? That Karl is the worst thing I
    can become?

JUDY
    He's a hater.

JIMMY
    Yeah? And?

JUDY
    Well in your own way … you're a hater too.

JIMMY
    There's a difference.

JUDY
    Is there.

JIMMY
    Yes there's a fucking difference. Surely you know,
    or if I'm actually talking to myself, I know or
    whoever the fuck I'm talking to, knows that there's
    a difference. He hates people. I … hate what
    people do … the things they do to each other. The
    lies they tell. The tribal beliefs they hold on to that
    support the lies … and make them do the things …
    the hateful things … they do. Well?

JUDY
    Well. Whatever. He hates. You hate. Hate is bad. (*to*
    DEREK) That sounds simple-minded enough to
    make me think I'm on the verge of an epiphany or

something. (*to JIMMY*) And that reminds me, given my ethno-religious cultural background, I'm in the wrong place.

JIMMY

Maybe you're not.

JUDY

What's that mean.

JIMMY

Maybe heaven's heaven.

JUDY

Like no. Have I seen any Jews? Any Muslims? I'm in Christian heaven buddy. I have been co-opted hook line and sinker. I joined a hymn sing last night. Guess what. I knew all the words. How'd that happen.

JIMMY

Don't blame me. You ever hear me singing any goddamn hymns?

JUDY

I bet it was your mother.

JIMMY

Oh yeah she snuck over and sung them into your ear while you were asleep.

JUDY

I bet that's exactly what she did, the evil bitch. But I forgive her. I forgive everyone. Except you.

JIMMY

Can't I just kill Karl. Can't I slit his fucking throat or something.

DEREK

Not if you wanna get to heaven, man.

JIMMY
You see, I gotta believe that's really me talking.
That "not if you wanna get to heaven" stuff. That's
that Catholic thing deep inside me ... (*to DEREK*)
Yeah you're me. (*to JUDY*) And so are you. You're
both me.

JUDY
Lucky us.

DEREK
Ask me something.

JIMMY
Whatya mean.

DEREK
All you gotta do is ask me how I feel about
something. Because you don't know shit about how
I feel about anything. So if I tell you something that
makes sense it's gotta be me.

JIMMY
Okay. Yeah. What's it like to be black.

DEREK
(*standing*) Fuck off. What kind of stupid question is
that.

JIMMY
I was just—

DEREK
Black when? Black anytime? Black now? Black with
a cop's gun up your ass? Yeah. Why don't I tell you
how it feels to be black and have a white cop
basically own you. It feels like shit. It feels like
you're eating shit. And it feels like you're always
gonna eat it. Three meals a day of shit. Then when
the cop says it's time you eat your last meal of shit,

then you die. (*looks at his safety suit*) This is fucked.
What's it about. Why am I wearing this thing. I
mean I think I saw a Formula One race on TV
once. Once. I remember thinking that looks cool.
So what's this. Is that the closest I got to having a
fucking dream. Is that the only thing I ever wanted
to be besides what I was. Which was some white
cop's bum boy. That's fucked. Really. (*sits, puts his
head down between his legs*) This is just a place where
you get to be fucked in a whole new way.

> *JUDY is moving to some music she hears in her head.*

JIMMY

Are you crying.

DEREK

What's it to you. I'm not giving you anymore
information about myself. Who are you to me.
Some guy who gave me nothing but grief. All that
Nubian shit. What was that about.

JIMMY

It was just ... me ... (*to JUDY*) He's sad. So ... What?
Heaven is a place where he gets ... to be sad?

> *JUDY takes off her doctor's gown. She is wearing a
> fancy dress underneath, circa 1940s. She is still
> moving gracefully. She sits next to DEREK. Sings softly
> to him.*

JUDY

(*singing*) Heaven. I'm in heaven.
And my heart beats so that I can hardly speak
And I seem to find the happiness I seek
When we're out together dancing cheek to cheek

> *DEREK is looking down as he begins to sing ... then
> slowly he looks up ... smiling a little.*

112

DEREK

    (*singing*) Heaven, I'm in heaven
    And the cares that hang around me through the
    week
    Seem to vanish like a gambler's lucky streak
    When we're out together dancing cheek to cheek

        DEREK stands. Peels off safety suit. Underneath, he is
        wearing a 1940s style tux.

        The music grows. An orchestrated version of the song.
        DEREK and JUDY come together. They begin to dance.
        They do the entire number beautifully.
        The music grows. They dance off.

        JIMMY lowers his head.
        Blackout.

Scene Nine

*JIMMY and DAVID both moving around in an
agitated manner.*

JIMMY

Whatya mean you don't know where she is.

DAVID

She left. She's left before, you know. It's just that
this time she didn't come back.

JIMMY

Whatya mean she's left before. I didn't know that.

DAVID

Why should you know that. You're never home
anymore. You're always here.

JIMMY

I gotta be here. People are looking for me here.

DAVID

What people.

JIMMY

People who need to find me.

DAVID

What are you talking about.

JIMMY

People. Some of them are living. Some of them are
dead.

DAVID

What's wrong with you. Have you been drinking.

JIMMY

I don't think you should be standing there
interrogating me like this. I think you should be
out looking for Sissy.

DAVID

What about you.

JIMMY

I told you! I'm needed here!

DAVID

You're needed at home. The place is a mess.
There's dust on everything.

JIMMY

Well dust then. Dust things. Can't you dust things.

DAVID

I don't have time. I already do all the cooking and
shopping.

JIMMY

How long's a little dusting take.

DAVID

Speaking of shopping. The kids both need new
shoes.

JIMMY

Yeah okay. Can't you take care of that.

DAVID

What about you.

JIMMY

I can't do that kind of stuff now. Don't you
understand.

DAVID

Understand what.

JIMMY

I can't be at home with the kids. It's wrong.

DAVID

How can it be wrong. They're your children.

JIMMY

Not them. The world. The world is wrong. How can I take care of them if I don't take care of the world first.

DAVID

What do you mean. What are you talking about.

JIMMY

Something's wrong. I have to fix it. Someone's ... doing ... something wrong. I have to fix it.

DAVID

People are wondering about me. I see them hanging around the parking lot across from the synagogue. Talking. I know they're asking each other "Why has he become a housekeeper for this man. A man who used to insult him in public."

JIMMY

Well just tell them that's all water under the bridge. Tell them we're ... forging a new relationship ... based on—

DAVID

Based on my cooking!

JIMMY

I think of you as a friend.

DAVID

No you don't. You think of me as someone who'll do all your dirty work for you. Talk to your children about things you find too painful to talk about.

JIMMY
Well that's what a friend would do. You're a friend.

DAVID
I don't feel like a friend.

JIMMY
Well that's your problem. Now can you just leave me alone. The people that need me to be here ... that I need to be here for ... might not come if ... I'm not alone.

DAVID
Why not.

JIMMY
Well suppose these people, no matter where they are now, are real and they're doing something that is very unusual for them to do only because they think I need to know something or see or hear something ... for whatever reason ... Okay but suppose they're not ... real ... then it's just about me ... and what I think and feel and need to see and hear ... So that I can ... ... you know ... fix things ... Either way it's better if I'm alone.

DAVID
I kept some dinner for you. We can heat it in the microwave. I think you should come home.

JIMMY
I can't.

DAVID
Why not.

JIMMY
I just told you!

DAVID
I didn't understand what you told me.

JIMMY

It's not important that you understand. If you want
something important to do, go look for Sissy.
Please. It's not safe out there. Just go look for her.
Okay?

DAVID

Yes. All right. (*starts off*) I'll put the kids to bed. I'll
call Judy's mother. She'll come over ... then I'll go
look for Sissy.

JIMMY

Thanks.

DAVID

I like her too.

JIMMY

I know you do.

DAVID

(*stopping*) Will you be all right.

JIMMY

I don't know.

> DAVID *looks at him. Leaves.*
> *A loud laugh.*

KARL

(*from behind a tree*) Faggot!!

> KARL *steps out from behind a tree.*

KARL

Hey what's goin' on with you guys. You talk like a
couple of old queens. It is truly the weirdest
fucking relationship I've ever spied on. "You do the
dusting, I can't do the dusting, I do the shopping."

JIMMY

I need to talk to you.

KARL

I guess you do, yeah.

JIMMY

I need to know if you were shitting me before.
About killing that kid ... About killing Judy ... And
if you were lying, why would you wanna fuck with
me like that. What kind of a—

KARL

I wasn't.

JIMMY

What.

KARL

I wasn't shitting you. I killed Judy. You gotta come
to grips with that Jimmy. That's something you're
just gonna have to deal with.

JIMMY

Are you the devil.

KARL

What.

JIMMY

I'm just asking. Are you Satan. Is this a test. Are you
Satan and are you testing me. Are we in a state of
suspended grace here. Is this some kind of
transition place between heaven and hell.

KARL

You mean like purgatory, Jimmy.

JIMMY

Like purgatory, yeah.

KARL

What the fuck is wrong with you.

JIMMY

Nothing. I'm just asking.

KARL reaches behind the tree. Pulls out a large duffel bag.

KARL

That was some weird shit you just said.

JIMMY

I was just asking. What's in the bag.

KARL

Guess.

JIMMY

What's in the goddamn bag!

KARL

I'll tell you what's in the goddamn bag when I'm ready to tell you what's in the goddamn bag.

JIMMY

I'll just look for myself then, okay?

JIMMY starts forward.
KARL takes out a gun.

KARL

No. It's not okay! I said I'd show you when I was fucking ready to show you! Now stand still or I'll shoot your pecker off.

JIMMY stops.

JIMMY

What's happened to you.

KARL

You happened to me. You happened to me that day at that goddamn hearing. We walk in there. Tommy and me. He's saying no sweat. Jimmy's in charge. He won't let them screw me. Jimmy's the guy. And he's one of us. Didn't we work all those years on the same assembly line. Didn't we go to the same church. Screw the same girls. So we're in good hands. But then you open your mouth and right away we know that's not who you are anymore. You're just some cocksuckin' government lawyer who wants our fucking heads. All that shit you talked. Those poor black kids. Those poor Asian kids. All those poor fucking kids from those poor families forced to join those fucking gangs. And then there's all those bad-hearted cops on top of that who want nothing else but to cause these kids grief and in some cases actually kill the poor little bastards ... So you screwed Tommy and Tommy killed himself and then I said to myself, "They wanna see a bad cop I'll show them a bad cop." So I started doing my things. Doing various ... things. You know ... killing ... things like that ... Wanna see what's in the bag? Say please.

JIMMY
Please.

KARL
No problem.

> KARL *unzips the bag. Takes an unconscious SISSY out by her hair.*

JIMMY
Is she ... dead.

KARL
Not yet.

JIMMY
Whatya want.

KARL
I want you to judge me, Jimmy. Not like in that hearing room. But face to face. Man to man. Like it should be. I want you to examine my deed and make me accountable if you can.

JIMMY

Which means what.

KARL

Well that'll be up to you what it means.

JIMMY

What'd you do to her.

KARL

She's a druggie, Jimmy. If you give her a drug, she takes it. She takes whatever you give her. If you give her too much, she takes too much.

JIMMY

So why. Why do something like that.

KARL

Why not.

JIMMY

Who was she hurting.

KARL

Who was she helping. Who the fuck is she anyway. What good is she. What good are any of them. Why can't they ... just die. What do they do with their lives. What do they provide that we're all gonna miss ... But you don't think that do you. You think she's really worth something ... How much. How much is she worth.

> KARL takes a knife out. Puts it to SISSY's throat. Tosses his gun toward JIMMY. It lands in front of JIMMY's feet.

KARL

Feel like saving a life today? All you gotta do is be the guy you used to be ... Right on the line, Jimmy. No bullshit. Just pick up the fucking gun and save this little druggie slut's life ... I'll slit her throat,

Jimmy. If you don't pick up the gun she's dead. Do
it!

> *JIMMY yells. Picks up the gun.*

KARL

Drop the knife! Drop the goddamn knife!!

> *KARL drops the knife.*

KARL

Oh. Oh my God. Jimmy ... (*he is crying*) ... Wait ...
don't ... Jimmy ... don't ... please ... (*he is crawling
towards JIMMY*) What's ... happened to me ... I'm so
scared ... God help me. I'm so ... fucking scared!

> *KARL takes another gun from his belt. Shoots JIMMY.*
> *JIMMY falls. Dead.*
> *KARL walks over to JIMMY. Looks down.*

KARL

As if. (*laughs*)

> *SISSY picks up the knife. Staggers to KARL. Plunges
> the knife in his back.*

KARL

Jesus Christ!!
> *KARL falls to his knees. Then falls forward. Dead.*
> *SISSY collapses. Starts to crawl off.*
> *A blinding white light. Music.*
> *JIMMY stands and slowly walks into the light.*
> *Music changes and KARL stands and is drawn into
> the light, beginning to disrobe as he does.*
> *Blackout.*

Scene Ten

JIMMY waiting ... looking around.
DEREK, dressed in rags, on bench.
DAVID leaning against a tree. Lost in thought.

ANNOUNCER

Ladies and gentlemen. Because he called out the
name of his lord just seconds before he died,
because he yelled in anguish and despair the name
of Jesus Christ, and to show it's never too late to do
that, here he is in heaven. Embraced and forgiven
and reborn in an everlasting way. You knew him as
Karl. But he'd like us all to call him ... Groovy Boy!!

Loud early seventies rock music. Try "Rubber Bullets"
by 10 C.C.

KARL comes down or out from heaven. He is dressed
in a tougher version of the cop from The Village
People. He is joined by two female dancers and they
do a brief exuberant number.

Note: In the Toronto production we disguised JUDY
and SISSY and they became the "Karlettes."

As the dance finishes the female dancers return to
heaven and KARL sits next to DEREK and smiles.
DEREK is just staring at him.

KARL

You seem hostile. There's a bad vibe going on
between us. And it's coming from you, Derek.

DEREK

You killed me.

KARL

That was then. This is now.

DEREK

I don't care. You made me feel like a pile of shit.
Then you blew my brains out.

KARL

Yeah. But this is heaven. I'm redeemed. I'm
redeemed in the name of Jesus Christ Our Lord.

DEREK

Yeah. How come.

KARL

Well I was killed too. And so because of that,
because I'm also in many ways a victim of the
terrible tribulations of the earthly world no matter
how you look at it, I am absolved of all my sins and
I am received into the arms of the Maker. I'm
reborn in the name of Jesus Christ Our Lord.

DEREK

Bullshit.

KARL

You mean amen, don't you. Look I'm sorry you
can't get your head around it, man. But everything
is cool with me now. Can't you tell. I feel fine. I
look at you and you don't make me want to vomit
or anything. I look at your skin for example and I
have nothing against it. It's ... just skin. Sure it's
different from mine. It's you know ... darker. But
I'm cool with that.

DEREK

Bullshit.

KARL

No. Honest. Hey I know I did some really bad stuff.
Stuff no one even wants to talk about around here.
Technically I shouldn't be in this place. I just made
it under the wire. I mean I thought I was yelling
"Jesus Christ" because that friggin' knife hurt so
much. But another spin got put on it and here I am.

DEREK

Fuck off.

KARL

Hey. This is heaven. I don't think you should be
telling me to fuck off.

DEREK

Fuck off.

KARL

What's wrong with you. Why's your vibe so hostile.
How come you're not feeling that warm glow you
get in the arms of Jesus Christ Our Lord.

DEREK

Because I'm not. I'm angry.

KARL

Angry? In heaven. Wow. That's heavy shit.

DEREK

Well look at me, asshole. Look at what I'm wearing.

KARL

Yeah? So?

DEREK

So? Oh fuck off.

KARL

It's okay. I forgive you.

DEREK

What. You gotta be kidding. Fuck right off!

KARL smiles. Shrugs.

KARL

This is really messing you up, isn't it. If I was still an evil man I'd think this is just about the worst thing I could do to you. If I wanted to ... you know ... destroy your soul, I'd manage somehow to get into heaven just so I could be near you like this ... And smile. (*smiles*) Like this.

DEREK just looks at him in disbelief.
Lights fade on KARL and DEREK.
Lights up on JUDY and JIMMY. They are snuggling.
JUDY mostly.

JIMMY

(*pointing at KARL*) See? Just like I always thought. Heaven is crap. It's a cool place for serial killers. They're the ones who need redemption. They get absolved and received into the arms of Jesus. But all people like Derek and me get from it is a feeling that we've been fucked yet again.

JUDY

You could try looking at it another way, you know ... You do get to be with me.

JIMMY

Nah. It's the same as before. I can't enjoy it. If everyone isn't invited, then the party stinks. Just like life. Like you were always asking me "What's your problem. Your life's okay. You've got a good job. A family that loves you. Why are you always so agitated?" Because I *was*. That's why. Because me having those things in a world where a lot of people didn't have anything just made me feel worse.

JUDY

> You know Jimmy, you could start over here.
> Remember. The theory is you get to be what you
> want. Deep down, in spite of everything, don't you
> just want to be happy anyway.

JIMMY

> No. I mean look at Derek. I'll be happy when he's
> happy. Which will be basically never. You know why?
> Because obviously this isn't just Christian heaven.
> It's white Christian heaven. Those are slave's
> clothes he's wearing. Why's he wearing slave
> clothes. Whose idea was that ... Come on. What
> insensitive clod comes up with the idea of putting
> the black guy in slave clothes. What's the fucking
> point of that. Who did this!?

> > *A spotlight on DAVID.*
> > *JIMMY walks over to DAVID. Stands behind him ...*
> > *talking into the back of his head ...*

JIMMY

> You really need to ask yourself what's goin' on in
> your mind there, David. You absolve the serial killer
> and you put the black guy in slave's clothes. This is
> your idea of heaven. And what's goin' on between
> me and Judy. You gonna just picture us nattering at
> each other for eternity? You're supposed to be a
> religious man. Some kind of spiritual component
> might be in order here, David.

> > *DAVID looks up.*

DAVID

> I'm not thinking of anything ... except you and
> Judy. Maybe you're the one thinking about those
> things. Maybe you're the one who put the black

man in slave's clothes. Maybe it's your guilt. Not mine. I'm not the only one with guilt around here.

JIMMY walks back to JUDY.

JIMMY

He didn't put him in the slaves clothes. This is pretty confusing. Do you think people in heaven can have other people in heaven as figments of their imagination.

JIMMY, JUDY, KARL and DEREK all look at each other.

JUDY

I think the whole thing might be built on that kind of delusion, don't you? What did he mean he's only thinking of us. What about us.

They turn to each other. Look each other up and down. Smile lasciviously. They speak the next section a little mechanically.

JUDY

I'm horny.

JIMMY

So am I.

JUDY

I've missed having sex with you.

JIMMY

I've missed having sex with you too. Do you want to do it now.

JUDY

Yes. Let's do it now.

JIMMY

Yes. Let's do it now. Let's do it hard and fast.

JUDY

Yes. Hard and fast. Then let's do it again and again.
Let's do it ... forever.

Pause.

*They both frown. Look at DAVID. Gesture "What is
this?"*

*Lights fade on JIMMY and JUDY and on KARL and
DEREK.*

DAVID starts to bang his head against the tree.

DAVID

Idiot. Stupid jealous man. They're dead for God's
sake. They can't have sex. God. I hate myself.

SISSY comes on. A bit cleaned up. On stilts.

SISSY

Hi.

DAVID

Hey. Look at you. You're back up there.

SISSY

Yeah well why not, I guess.

DAVID

No that's wonderful. You should do it everyday. It'll
help you recover. Did you get the kids off to school.

SISSY

Yeah. Eventually. We had a big fight about their
lunches. Like I'm supposed to know when they're
tired of something.

DAVID

Well we do our best, right.

SISSY

Yeah I suppose, but I don't really get what's goin'
on. It's like we're raising those kids or something.

DAVID

I think the grandparents are going to take them
soon. I'm sure one of the grandmothers will
definitely want them.

SISSY

Yeah well they don't seem in any fucking hurry.
And in the meantime it's just us. The rabbi and the
heroin addict.

DAVID

You're not a heroin addict. You're on methadone.

SISSY

I'm on methadone because I'm a heroin addict ...
Anyway it's pretty weird, this little family we've got
there. It can't just go on forever, can it.

DAVID

I don't know.

SISSY

Why were you banging your head before.

DAVID

Oh it's just a habit. (*he shrugs*) I'm worried Judy is
in heaven having sexual relations with James. That's
all I've got on my mind, and it's driving me crazy.
Pathetic. I'm pathetic.

SISSY

No. You're just jealous.

DAVID

I should be better than that. Why can't I have
better thoughts about them than that.

SISSY

Why should you.

DAVID

Hey. Come on. I'm a rabbi.

SISSY

What's that mean. You're just a guy, David. Really.
Give yourself a break. Hey, watch this.

She makes some fancy move on the stilts.

DAVID

Amazing.

SISSY

Yeah really. With all the junk I've got in my system.

DAVID

I think there's a reason you're good at these things.
There's a purpose in it.

SISSY

Yeah? What.

DAVID

I don't know. But it could be revealed.

SISSY

You mean by God? Come on David, I don't believe
in God.

DAVID

No? Well why should you. (*shrugs*) Why should you.

SISSY

I don't believe in anything really … Except maybe
you. The way you're taking care of everything … So
if you're doing that because you believe in God
then, I don't know, maybe I should try to believe
too. Whatya think.

DAVID

I think you should just believe in yourself. I think
that would be the better choice. Under the
circumstances. Considering the precarious nature
of your life, I wouldn't take a chance that anything

or anyone ... you know bigger ... is going to intervene in a helpful way.

SISSY

What are you saying there, David. It sounds like you don't really believe in God either.

DAVID

I try hard to believe. I get by mostly just by trying. But in your position I can't honestly advise you to go that way. Don't tell anyone.

SISSY

I don't know anyone. Listen. That night Jimmy and Karl the cop got killed ... That night I came home all messed up ... I was mostly out of it because Karl had overdosed me ... But I remember enough. I remember that I killed him.

DAVID

Really.

SISSY

He killed Jimmy. And I think he killed Derek too. I had to do it. It felt ... right. Don't turn me in okay. I don't wanna go to prison. I don't think I'd do so good there.

Pause.

DAVID

Well they probably wouldn't let you bring your stilts.

SISSY

I just needed to tell someone.

DAVID

I understand. Do you want to talk about it.

SISSY

I just did … But the thing is we gotta make a deal.
If I don't tell anyone you're a rabbi who tries to
believe in God but really doesn't, then you can't
tell anyone I killed that cop, Okay?

DAVID

Seems fair.

SISSY

Watch!

> *She does some other fancy thing on the stilts. Takes
> out her hackysacks and begins to juggle.*

DAVID

Amazing.

SISSY

So how come you believe in heaven.

DAVID

What do you mean.

SISSY

You said you were thinking about them having sex
in heaven. You don't believe in God but you still
believe in heaven. That's weird, David.

DAVID

Well … Yes. It is.

SISSY

Watch.

> *She begins to juggle.*
> *Lights down on DAVID.*

SISSY

I don't know why this feels so good.

> *Hold on SISSY in a spotlight. Then lights down on
> her too. The balls she is juggling glow in the dark.
> Blackout.*

JIMMY in a spotlight. In front of a microphone.
Dressed more or less as he was at the beginning of the
play.
A smattering of recorded applause. Canned laughter
fading out.
There is a glass of water on a stool.

JIMMY

Yeah, thanks. But where was I. Oh yeah. Pain. It's
all about pain. Unbearable soul-sucking pain. And
what we do to escape it. But first, speaking of
sucking. And this might be related to pain. But
anyway when I was a teenager I was busted for
possession and somehow I managed to keep my
parents from finding out. And I go to court by
myself to take whatever enlightened punishment is
gonna be doled out to me for the mortal sin of
having two reefers in my jean jacket. But because
I'm nervous and my cure for that was always to get
pretty wasted, I take some mescaline I've had
stashed away for awhile and I find myself sitting at
the back of the courtroom, my mind drifting
towards the outskirts of reality. Sweating. Vibrating.
And then suddenly a voice from the front
announces that some guy's been charged with
sucking on a cannibal's dick. And immediately a
whole bunch of stuff races through my head. First.
Why is that a crime. Second. Why wasn't I told that
cannibals were living around here. And also, if this
guy really was a cannibal wouldn't sucking on his
dick be kind of a dangerous thing to do. As in,
"Thanks for the blowjob. Boy am I ever hungry."
Anyway I'm tormenting myself with all these
questions when somehow it gets through the
matted fucking mess which is my brain that the guy

is actually being charged with marijuana use. And that some uptight narc has been up there describing this horror as "sucking on a cannabis stick." Okay so I've got that straight now. But I'm haunted by my initial response. And the image of a huge black man getting blown by this pimply undergraduate in the defendant's seat. First why is the guy in my brain black. And second why is he huge. And the only answer I can come up with is … I must be a racist. I begin to cry. In complete and utter shame. I'm an ignorant fucking bigot. Just like my dad and my uncles and just about everyone I've ever known. I give up. I've tried to be better. But what's the use. Sure, two of my best friends in school are black and another one is a subversive little genius from Korea. But basically deep in my soul I'm a white supremacist. And I'm gonna have to learn to live with that. I'm given a five hundred dollar fine and told never to do it again. And meanwhile, back at my high school the authorities are busy breaking into my locker to look for the rest of my illicit stash. An illegal action that incenses me to this day. Anyway they don't find any drugs. Because I don't keep my fucking drugs in my fucking school locker. What am I a fucking idiot. All they find are two bottles of homemade wine my friend Rocco stole from his father and a Molson's two-four. But apparently that's reason enough to inform my parents that I'm a serious substance abuser, and I'm placed in "protective counselling" for the rest of my high school years. Which means basically that I was watched. I was watched very closely. But that was okay. Because I was watching myself. I was watching myself for any

136

hint of the incipient Nazism. Any sign at all that not only was I intolerant of minorities but that I actually wanted them eradicated from the face of the earth. And in university I signed up for every black studies course I could find. I took women's studies. I tried to learn Cantonese. For three years in a row I rode a float in the Gay Pride Parade with a lit candle shoved up my ass. People would ask me what it meant. I mean I was surrounded by dozens of naked guys with dildos they were trying to stick in every orifice they could find. And they wanted to know about the candle. "It doesn't mean anything. I'm just doing what you're doing!! Trying to get attention!" I sought out summer jobs and part-time jobs that were usually only offered to non-English speaking immigrants. I needed to know I liked these people. That I could live and work with these people ... I picked worms. For seven weeks one summer I stood on a street corner with fifty Greek women waiting for a truck to pick us up and drive us to a golf course to pick worms at sundown. Big juicy dew worms good for catching perch and pickerel. We were given miner's lamps to strap around our heads and tin cans to strap around our legs just above the knee and we worked like dogs picking worms till dawn for piss-poor money the driver basically threw at us while he was depositing us back on the street corner. I worked at bonding with those Greek women even though every single one of them hated my guts from the moment they laid eyes on me because they thought the only reason a guy like me would be doing a sad demeaning job like this was for sex. But I didn't want to fuck them. I wanted to be one of them.

Yeah in essence I wanted to be a female Greek immigrant worm-picker and nothing else. But I couldn't tell them that. I couldn't tell anyone. Because no one would ... understand. So anyway I'm working away integrating myself, my conscious self, and therefore I hope, my unconscious self too, into the entire human family. I leave the Ford assembly line after eight years. I go to law school. I graduate. I do legal aid work for any person of colour I can find. I don't care if they're guilty. I don't care what they've done. Or how many times they've done it. I try my best to fuck the system and get them off. I think I'm helping. I'm happy. And then just about the best thing that can happen to someone who's worried that he might be a subconscious Nazi slimeball, happens to me. I fall in love with a Jew. It's amazing. I am smitten by one of the chosen and my family goes into collective massive cardiac arrest. This makes me positively giddy and when we get married and no one from my family shows up and no one from her family shows I feel nothing except elation. Because they're the fucking racists and I'm a fucking complete human being. And when I hear what her father thinks of me ... words like loser and moron are thrown around freely, I feel great ... I mean I guess he didn't know I'd be a featured act here at the Celestial Improv. Yeah God thinks I'm funny. And the feeling's mutual. Anyway the more abuse our relatives hurled at us, the better I felt. In fact I'd never felt better in my life. And at work which was now a position on a fancy new Human Rights Commission designed to basically get all the nattering do-gooders off the government's back. I was the one true light of moral indignation. On behalf of every person of every colour from every corner of the world I stood and pounded out justice. I arranged for all sorts of companies to be fined for failing to implement pay equity and for unjust dismissal often based, they said, on inadequate language skills. And I'd scream "You're fucking right she has a little trouble with English. Whatya expect. Can you speak Farsi? Not a fucking word I bet. So shut up. And sign her paycheque you racist pig!" And of course many of these employers *were* racists. And lots of other people whose names came to my attention were racists. Cops. Teachers. 911 operators who patronized or ignored anyone with a Jamaican accent. They were all racists to me. And I was a fucking saint. And the people on whose behalf I worked, the poor, the disenfranchised, they were, well, the inheritors of the earth as far as I was concerned. Except I didn't know shit about the people on whose behalf I worked. Just like I didn't know anything about my two black friends in school. Or the Korean genius either. I wasn't a racist, I'd pretty much settled that in my mind, but I wasn't anything good either. I was just a guy who … didn't know shit. Which brings us back to pain. (*takes a sip of water*) You wanna talk about pain? I'll give you pain. Okay here we are in blissful eternity, you're probably thinking, and this guy wants to talk about pain. What's his problem. Well, okay, but heaven or no heaven you gotta think what happens on earth is kinda worth remembering. And when people suffer, the response to that suffering has to be better than "it's all gonna be all right in heaven."

Okay you know what? Forget pain. Let's talk about bullshit. Eternal bullshit. Bullshit in heaven even as it is on earth. Here's the problem I have with heaven. Who needs it. And also who asked for it. When I was a kid and some priest put his hand lovingly on my knee and said something like, "Be a good boy and you'll get to heaven." All I remember thinking is, "No fucking way." I'm not going anywhere where you think you're gonna be too. In fact, everyone I ever heard talking about heaven scared the shit out of me. Or annoyed me so much I wanted to rip their face off ... As far as entry into the sweet hereafter being used as an incentive for people to behave better on earth, well what an odious paternalistic idea that is. I mean if you really need incentives why not just get, you know, real. I'm thinking of this cable TV channel that was looking for someone to host a new call-in talk show. Now this is one of those new be-a-better-person channels. You know, they all have names like Life or Discovery, or Vision or some kind of crap like that ... Anyway, they call this guy in for an interview. An acerbic, intolerant prick. One of those right wing "I'm doing fine so fuck you" assholes. A guy who thinks all women should stay home with the kids except his woman who has a great job as an editor for a large magazine. Which really means he thinks only women from the lower classes should stay home with the kids. The disgusting hypocrite. Anyway they say to this guy, "The thing is, we're one of those be a better person channels so if we give you this job you gotta promise to be ... a better person." So he asks what the salary is. And they tell him. And it's quite a lot of money. And the guy says "No problem. I was just waiting for an incentive." ... So I'm thinking if God wants people on earth to think and behave in a better way, why doesn't God just offer them money. That's real. That'd work. It'd work on a whole bunch of levels. First desperately poor people would have money and stop behaving so fucking ... desperately ... Next well the better behaviour stuff would have obvious benefits ... But most important to me ... we'd be able to knock off all that bullshit about redemption and guilt and all that other terrifying superstitious garbage. (*shrugs*) Talk about painful stuff. (*shrugs*)

Anyway ... (*takes a sip of water*) My wife got killed. She was carrying our unborn child ... That was a drag ... (*lights start to fade*) And yeah ... well I'm sorry but that takes me right back to that pain thing. I mean okay I'm ... here in heaven but really am I just supposed to forget that happened ... I mean talk about insensitive ... I mean I guess we'll take just about any fucking excuse to feel good. (*shrugs*) Like that helps or something. Like feeling good is the ... most important thing ... or something. (*shrugs*)

Blackout.

The End